SPIRITUALITY

BY

GREGORY J. FERNANDEZ JR.

ISBN # 978-0-557-30672-5

Cover Photo by Ilya Petushkov

Who among you is wise and understanding? Let him show by his good behavior his deeds in the gentleness of wisdom. But if you have bitter jealousy and selfish ambition in your heart, do not be arrogant and so lie against the truth. This wisdom is not that which comes down from above, but is earthly, natural, demonic. For where jealousy and selfish ambition exist, there is disorder and every evil thing. But the wisdom from above is first pure, then peaceable, gentle, reasonable, full of mercy and good fruits, unwavering, without hypocrisy. And the seed whose fruit is righteousness is sown in peace by those who make peace. **James 3:13-18**

TABLE OF CONTENTS

INTRODUCTION

REVELATIONS 22:16 I, Jesus, have sent my angel to give you this testimony for the churches. I am the root and the offspring of David, and the bright morning star.

Trouble
When I'm in trouble,
and when I'm in need,
I turn to the Lord,
For in faith I believe,
For man is a sinner,
Who's path is destruction,
Through faith and through prayer,
God can make me something,
I try and I fail,
So I try, try again,
I have faith his existence,
Is real, not pretend,
For God is the kingdom,
His power unstoppable,
Have faith and believe,
With God, anything is possible.

REVELATIONS 19:11 And I saw Heaven opened, and behold a white horse; and he that sat upon him was called Faithful and True, and in righteousness he [does] judge and make war.

What's the point in reading the Bible if you don't have faith that it is the word of God? If you do not believe the Bible is the word of God, isn't it easy to assume *it's just another book*? What separates the Bible from every other spiritual book?

"And? So what? What makes them so sure that the Bible is the word of God?"

EPHESIANS 3:7-12 I became a servant of this gospel by the gift of God's grace given me through the working of his power. Although I am less than the least of all God's people, this grace was given me: to preach to the Gentiles the unsearchable riches of Christ, and to make plain to everyone the administration of this mystery, which for ages past was kept hidden in God, who created all things. His intent was that now, through the church, the manifold wisdom of God should be made known to the rulers and authorities in the heavenly realms, according to his eternal purpose which he accomplished in Christ Jesus our Lord. In him and through faith in him we may approach God with freedom and confidence.

What is the one thing every church has in common today? What is the one thing we can be sure to find inside of our local church? The Bible. How do we know that the Bible is the living word of God? It says so. How do we know that the information inside of the Bible is accurate? I believe it because I have read the Bible. I believe it because God has worked miracles in my life. I believe that God has provided me with everything I need in life, and more, because of my belief that Jesus Christ is Lord, and that I try to follow what God would have me do (based on what the Bible teaches we should be, ambassadors and servants of Jesus Christ). Faith is a blessing that the evil one tries to make you doubt. For even the evil one knows the power of faith. So the righteous people strive to keep the faith. Jesus Christ told Thomas that since Thomas saw the holes in the hands of Jesus Christ, he believed that Christ had risen from the grave. Jesus Christ stresses how more blessed people will be who have not seen the Christ, yet still believe.

JOHN 20:24-29 Now Thomas (called Didymus), one of the twelve, was not with the disciples when Jesus came. So the other disciples told him, "We have seen the Lord!" But he said to them, "Unless I see the nail marks in his hands and put my finger where the nails were, and put my hand into his side, I will not believe it."

A week later his disciples were in the house again, and Thomas was with them. Though the doors were locked, Jesus came and stood among them and said, "**Peace be with you!**" Then he said to Thomas, "**Put your finger here; see my hands. Reach out your hand and put it into my side. Stop doubting and believe.**"

Thomas said to him, "My Lord and my God!"

Then Jesus told him, "**Because you have seen me, you have believed; blessed are those who have not seen and yet have believed.**"

If we do not believe that the Bible is the word of God, what's the point of reading it? When we seek God, what is the common denominator in our quest? The Bible. What will lead you to know and understand God and what his purpose is for this world? The Bible. If you are not reading the Bible, yet are seeking God, what type of God are you seeking? Is it the same God as in the Bible? Or is it a god that you are creating in your own head? A narcissist would take what they like inside the Bible and leave out what they don't like. In essence, they create their own version of god. Sounds more like a cult to me. To understand God, to seek God, to learn about God, your journey should include the Bible. This book should be a big part of your spiritual search. How can you look up to Heaven, how can you pray, how can you follow Jesus without reading the Bible?

Yes, it can be a very difficult book to understand. For beginners, I would always suggest reading the New International Version of the Bible, as I did (or any version that is easy to read for you). The interpretation may be a little different, but it's essentially the same as the King James Version; it's easier for me to understand. Having read the NIV Bible, I am now trying to read the KJV Bible. The NIV Bible was handed to me when I was about 14. It meant a lot to me then. Yet over the years, as my spirituality weakened, the value I once had in this book diminished to the point that, somehow, it ended up in my older brother's hands for years.

Two years ago, I felt myself really wanting to get this Bible back from my brother, as it has sentimental value to me. My brother willingly gave me the Bible without any trouble. He never questioned why I wanted it back after so many years. That was a stand-up move. I began to wonder if asking him for it was selfish. Why did I really want it back? I had other Bibles, but it wasn't the same. Was my faith in a book, or in the Bible? If it was in the Bible, then shouldn't I be happy with any Bible? This particular Bible reminds me of a time when my spirituality was at an all time high, as well as when it was at an all time low.

When I was 14, I didn't appreciate the person who gave me that Bible, even though my name was imprinted on the cover. It is a beautiful leather bound black book, complete with a cardboard case. My friend's mom gave me this book for my birthday one year, after I got saved at their church.

I didn't take care of it. It boiled in the heat in the back of my car, until it was wedged under my passenger seat with a lot of useless papers, rotten fruit, and bread crumbs. It sat in a file cabinet for years. It was bent and creased, accompanied with coffee stains that are still there. Yet the words inside of this book would change my life, time and time again. It is still changing me today. This book is more than a gift or a leather book to me. It is the word of God. It is where I go to when I am lost. It's where I turn to when I am seeking. It is where I study the facts of God, in my spiritual quest to be closer to God. My spiritual journey may not begin or end with the Bible, but this book is the bulk of my spiritual journey. When you're writing an essay, or a report for class, what do you do? You research, looking for evidence, for facts, to support your thesis. God is no different. If you want to learn about God, where do you look? What historical evidence do we have in this modern day and age to understand God?

Am I beating a dead horse by now? There was a time when I thought researching 9/11 would be the most important thing I would ever do. That is, until I began to work at Family Radio. Though many different people could interpret the Bible differently, they were all seeking to be closer to God, to follow his word and to live a life devoted to Christ. They all had the same resource, *they all had the Bible*. Some people get turned off because there are so many versions and interpretations of the Bible that it boggles the mind. Don't give up! The more confused you get, the closer you are. The devil is a master of confusion. The devil will try to confuse you in anything you do, especially if it's seeking God. Don't let him win. Say a silent prayer to God, asking for wisdom, for guidance, for understanding and you will receive it. All you need is faith, will power, and determination.

Perseverance

"When people are born again, negative stubbornness turns into positive perseverance."

Being stubborn is not a good thing. So when it comes to believing in God, I have tried to turn my stubbornness into positive perseverance. Reading the Bible is the first step. Living your life the way Jesus Christ wants us to is the next step. Staying in this mindset is the hard part. To know Christ it's important to read the Bible, to discuss the Bible with others and to reach out and help others, just as Jesus would do.

I can't heal you with the touch of my finger, but I know someone who can. God has changed my life. Jesus Christ took my pain, my suffering, my guilt, my sins, and has turned them into ***fuel*** in order to humble myself, throw away my pride and follow Christ.

Pride

My pastor once said that the devil is the prince of pride. Well if that's true, then I want nothing to do with pride. Then I look at Jesus Christ. I turn to the scriptures to answer the question, how did Jesus feel about pride? Did Christ have pride? Did Christ think it was a good thing? To date, I have found no such evidence that Jesus encourages pride. Yet pride is a big part of our society today. What does Jesus teach about pride? The Pharisee were prideful in their meticulous ways, though they may have felt they were doing God's will.

It was their pride that blinded them. This blindness might have kept them from seeing the Christ right in front of their eyes. In this pride, they killed the son of God. Even if they, later on, *did* believe Jesus was the Christ, their pride would not allow them to admit this, even though they witnessed the Saints, that Jesus rose from the grave, walking in their synagogues. To this day, there are still many who do not believe that Jesus is the Christ. They have faith that he is not. Only God knows the answers I seek. So that is were I am seeking answers in my life. Through faith, understanding, and trials, we find peace, because through faith, we find God.

Why Fear The Devil?

"*Why should you fear? Why should you be afraid? Do you not know that the prince of this world has been judged? He is no lord, no prince any more. You have a different, a stronger Lord, Christ, who has overcome and bound him. Therefore let the prince and god of this world look sour, bare his teeth, make a great noise, threaten, and act in an unmannerly way; he can do no more than a bad dog on a chain, which may bark, run here and there, and tear at the chain. But because it is tied and you avoid it, it cannot bite you. So the devil acts toward every Christian.*

Therefore everything depends on this that we do not feel secure but continue in the fear of God and in prayer; then the chained dog cannot harm us. But this chained dog may at least frighten him who would be secure and go ahead without caution, although he may not come close enough to be bitten..." - **Martin Luther**

Christian

ROMANS 10:6-15 But the righteousness that is by faith says: "Do not say in your heart, 'Who will ascend into heaven?'" (that is, to bring Christ down) "or 'Who will descend into the deep?'" (that is, to bring Christ up from the dead). But what does it say? "The word is near you; it is in your mouth and in your heart," that is, the word of faith we are proclaiming: That if you confess with your mouth, "Jesus is Lord," and believe in your heart that God raised him from the dead, you will be saved. For it is with your heart that you believe and are justified, and it is with your mouth that you confess and are saved. As the Scripture says, "Anyone who trusts in him will never be put to shame." For there is no difference between Jew and Gentile—the same Lord is Lord of all and richly blesses all who call on him, for, "Everyone who calls on the name of the Lord will be saved."

How, then, can they call on the one they have not believed in? And how can they believe in the one of whom they have not heard? And how can they hear without someone preaching to them? And how can they preach unless they are sent? As it is written, "How beautiful are the feet of those who bring good news!"

As my Mother-in-law pointed out, ***you have to believe that you are a child of God.*** I didn't understand that until she told me.

John 20:31 But these are written that you may believe that Jesus is the Christ, the Son of God, and that by believing you may have life in his name.

John 3:36 Whoever believes in the Son has eternal life, but whoever rejects the Son will not see life, for God's wrath remains on him.

John 1:12-13 Yet to all who received him, to those who believed in his name, he gave the right to become children of God. Children born not of natural descent, nor of human decision or a husband's will, but born of God.

God's Condition

John 3:16 For God so loved the world that He gave His only begotten Son, that whoever believes in Him should not perish but have everlasting life. For God did not send His Son into the world to condemn the world, but that the world through Him might be saved.

John 3:18 He who believes in Him is not condemned; but he who does not believe is condemned already, because he has not believed in the name of the only begotten Son of God.

Acts 16:30-31 And brought them out, and said, Sirs, what must I do to be saved?And they said, Believe on the Lord Jesus Christ, and thou shalt be saved, and thy house.

Romans 10:9 That if thou shalt confess with thy mouth the Lord Jesus, and shalt believe in thine heart that God hath raised him from the dead, thou shalt be saved.

2 Corinthians 5:20-21 We are therefore Christ's ambassadors, as though God were making his appeal through us. We implore you on Christ's behalf: Be reconciled to God. God made him who had no sin to be sin for us, so that in him we might become the righteousness of God.

1Timothy 2:5 For there is one God, and one mediator between God and men, the man Christ Jesus; Who gave himself a ransom for all, to be testified in due time.

Romans 10:1-4 For Christ is the end of the law for righteousness to every one that believeth.

God's Guarantees

Philipians 3:9 And be found in him, not having mine own righteousness, which is of the law, but that which is through the faith of Christ, the righteousness which is of God by faith.

Romans 9:31-32 But Israel, which followed after the law of righteousness, hath not attained to the law of righteousness. Wherefore? Because they sought it not by faith, but as it were by the works of the law.

John 5:24 Most assuredly, I say to you, he who hears My word and believes in Him who sent Me has everlasting life, and shall not come into judgment, but has passed from death into life.

I don't claim to have ***all*** the answers as to how to get to Heaven and what one must do to ensure you're going there after you die. Only God knows for sure. I know where we can find clues and answers as to how to get there. I know where we can go to try and make sure we get to Heaven. But no one should say that someone else is ***not*** going to Heaven, unless they claim to be God. How dare we do this! We don't know. Only God knows.

Even with Judas, the one who betrayed Jesus Christ, it is speculated that he went to hell. Yet when I read the actual scripture in Acts, it clearly states that Judas "went to his own place." It does not say this place is hell. Yet I have always assumed that he went to hell. I had to seek for myself in order to understand that no one knows where exactly Judas Iscariot's "place is." Only God knows for certain. The rest is human speculation. It's sinners judging sinners. That is deception and pride, both of which are products of the devil.

ACTS 1:24-25 And they prayed and said, "You, Lord, who know the hearts of all, show which one of these two you have chosen, to take the place in this ministry and apostleship from which Judas turned aside to go to his own place."

Scriptures can be used to manipulate people. Scriptures can be used to guide people. Whatever the case, scriptures are being used. So for you to understand when you're being manipulated or tricked, you must try to understand scriptures yourself and not trust how another person interprets the Bible. It's ok to question your pastor, some pastors encourage it. As a Christian, I love to be challenged with scripture. Not because I want to prove I'm right, but because I know that this will help me grow as a Christian (if I truly am), and it will help me understand another point of view on how they interpret the Bible and why (whether I agree with it or not).

Baby Ruth

The book of Ruth in the Bible is a difficult book to understand, for me. I battled with reading this book and when I finished (it's only 4 pages long) I felt like I had just watched an episode of Seinfeld...*nothing happened.*

Recently, my pastor at East Hills Community Church in Oakland, California, asked us at the church to read the book of Ruth and e-mail him any questions we had. I jumped at the opportunity. I love asking people questions about the Bible, in order to understand the book better for myself. I don't understand a lot of things in this book. The more I read, the more questions I have. The more I read, the more my spiritual eyes begin to open. The more I read, the better I understand the Bible. So after I finished reading Ruth, I wrote him with some questions I had:

RE: ***THE BOOK OF RUTH***

Hey Scott. Clearly the spirit is not with me today. I wasn't sure what the point of these scriptures were? Am I missing something? Is the whole point of this book to describe the lineage of David? My first thought (and not my last on this subject) was is this an episode from Seinfeld? "Nothing happens!"

Obviously that's not the case. I can't imagine this being part of the Bible for nothing. Reading this is in one word, "depressing." Ok, all the men die and the women are left to beg for food by 'gleaning.' It took me long enough to figure out what gleaning was. Naomi sells the land of Elimelech, instead of taking it for herself, which I'm assuming is forbidden.

Then "Boaz takes Ruth" and (though not by blood relation?) Ruth has a child with a relative of her husband. Did men really take up deceased wives in order to "raise up the name of the deceased?" or was it something more sinful? Was this commanded by God? This just reinforces how little I know, and how little I understand about the Old Testament. This is another reason why when trying to get someone to pick up the Bible for the first time, I never, ever suggest a book from the Old Testament. The questions I have only show me how much I have to learn, grow and seek truth. If I find anything in the Bible depressing, it's got more to do with me and my personal situation (or a bad day) than with scripture. As you know, we can read scripture one day and be baffled and confused...some time later we can reread that same scripture and it makes perfect sense.

QUESTION #1 - Were men allowed to have multiple wives? Or is this man Boaz single? He has maidens. What is their relationship to Boaz?

QUESTION #2 - When Jesus preached to the people and spoke to his disciples, do the marriage rules of the book of Ruth contradict what Jesus taught? Is this one of those things Jesus came back to correct in the Old Testament?

QUESTION #3 - RUTH 4:17 says "a son has been born to Naomi" I thought it was Ruth?

Sincerely, Greg Fernandez Jr.

Terrific questions Greg, way to engage and think. I know what you mean about not suggesting an Old Testament book, it takes some digging,

digging that people rarely take the time to do. As you know having written your books and researched and presented your ideas, people might not always hear your premise and then say, "Hey, you're right!" In this book there are many many cultural items that I really should have prepared people better for. I am taking your comment - Nothing Happens - which made me smile ;) as a personal challenge to excellence in digging and getting to the bottom of this book. It is my hope that by the end of the book, God might make it one of your favorites and that it would give you a hunger for other OT books. Not only that, but I learn plenty from Seinfeld ... ;)

ROMANS 9:15-21 For he says to Moses, "I will have mercy on whom I have mercy, and I will have compassion on whom I have compassion." It does not, therefore, depend on man's desire or effort, but on God's mercy. For the Scripture says to Pharaoh: "I raised you up for this very purpose, that I might display my power in you and that my name might be proclaimed in all the earth." Therefore God has mercy on whom he wants to have mercy, and he hardens whom he wants to harden.

One of you will say to me: "Then why does God still blame us? For who resists his will?" But who are you, O man, to talk back to God? "Shall what is formed say to him who formed it, 'Why did you make me like this?'" Does not the potter have the right to make out of the same lump of clay some pottery for noble purposes and some for common use?

CHAPTER ONE
IT'S ABOUT "NOTHING"

EZEKIEL 13:3 Thus saith the Lord GOD; Woe unto the foolish prophets, that follow their own spirit, and have seen nothing!

My brother, Manny Fernandez, was beginning to think that perhaps the man he voted for, Barack Obama, was not the man he thought he was voting for. So many campaign promises turned out to be complete lies (sending our troops home in 18 months). Some time ago, my brother sent me a text asking, "What's it all for?" I believe he was referring to life, but it could have been towards something more political.

After thinking about it for a few weeks, I wondered what the bickering and debating in congress was about. I liken it to people putting on a TV show...

"What's the show about?"

"It's about *nothing*...everybody's doing something, we'll do nothing."

Doesn't that sound like what congress has been doing for the last fifty plus years when it comes to inflation, fiat currency and the health care system of the United States?

"They literally walk into a Chinese restaurant, can't get a table and nothing happens!" Sounds familiar to me. We let China and other countries buy our dollars, our Federal Reserve notes and wait for something positive to happen. Well, foreign countries start buying up the American infrastructure and as for good, hard working Americans? Nothing happens, nothing positive anyways.

"Well something happens!" says Jerry Seinfeld.

Well, Jerry, something happens when the people make it happen. Unfortunately, it's usually not something positive, constructive or good for the people. But enough of my negativity.

"What did you do today?"

"I got up and came to work."

"There's a show, that's a show."

"How is that a show?"

In a Democratic Republic, which is what America is, if nothing happens, then are we really a Democratic Republic? Am I a still a bodybuilder if I stop working out? Am I truly a president if I get into office and do *nothing*...and nothing constructive happens? What happened to America?

The separation between church and state was put in the United States Constitution to ensure the freedom to worship whoever or whatever you want. Why do people call America a Christian nation? We're not all Christians. Am I truly a Christian if I do nothing to grow as a Christian? If nothing happens to further my growth, what type of a Christian am I?

The Style of Jeans

What's your style? "My style? You could call it the art of fighting without fighting." - ***Bruce Lee***

My wife recently bought a pair of jeans. Most likely from Macy's. Any hoot, she was wearing them one day and I couldn't help but notice several rips in her jeans. So I asked her, "What happened?"

"That's how they're made," was her response.

"You mean to tell me you paid good hard earned money on a pair of ripped and faded jeans?" It didn't make sense to me.

She recently bought me a very comfortable pair of light blue jeans. They're my favorites pair. I wore them so much in such sort a time that they ripped in the knee cap area. I was a little upset, since they were brand new. I figured since she had a pair of ripped jeans, I could have a pair too. Maybe people would think she bought them from Macy's too? There was just one difference. She had the confidence to wear the ripped jeans and feel comfortable. I did not. I began to feel self-conscious within an hour of having them on and going out in public. I felt like a homeless person or something. Perhaps I am not as confident as I would like to be.

I'd like to tell you that I did not mind wearing the ripped jeans. I'd love to tell you that clothes mean very little to me. Yet when I put on a pair of slacks, a dress shirt, and my leather jacket, I feel the confidence oozing from My blood. Why is that? With God as my Shepherd, I should feel comfortable in anything...but I don't.

Where does this uncomfortable feeling stem from? As I look up to Heaven, I am reminded of what's important in this life and what is not. Ripped jeans are not important. My search for Heaven is. My search began when I was born, without me knowing it at the time. My search ends when I die. So while I am alive, how can I further my search? What resource has

God 'left behind' for me to actively continue my search?

The Bible.

My style in life is the style of no style. I wear what feels comfortable, what God gives me, and what is usually on sale. Am I cheap? Perhaps to some people, but a trend is just me copying someone else. To have your own style is having the style of no style; if you slap a label on your own style, it becomes your style, which can turn into a trend. Confused? In a fast paced world like ours, the best way to find peace, to remain calm, is to stop and think...deeply.

Compared to finding and studying the word of God, style is meaningless. When God is the most important thing in your life, style looses its substance. As your own 'meaning of life' becomes clear, worldly materialistic goods carry less value. Style is a frame of mind. So what's your style?

Better Than Me?

"You think you're better than me don't you?"

"What? You think you're better than *him*?"

"Look, for the record, I think you're all better than me, ok?"

"Alright then."

Like the old song, "My mind is playin' tricks on me," our thoughts can be deceiving. Our assumptions can be very damaging to any relationships we have. This is why communication is so important.

"Your thoughts betray you."

Confusion

The devil is the master of confusion,
The deception he breeds is all but an illusion,
The Lord is the master of our souls,
We call on God when life is tough and the earth is cold.

I have been searching for the kingdom of Heaven all my life.

MATHEW 13:31-32 The Kingdom of Heaven is like to a grain of mustard seed, which a man took, and sowed in his field:

Which indeed is the least of all seeds: but when it is grown, it is the greatest among herbs, and becometh a tree, so that the birds of the air come and lodge in the branches thereof.

“The least of all seeds,” puts me in my place. I am not greater, nor lesser than anyone. As with all humans, I am sin. It's the battle within that will decide my fate. I can't worry if someone thinks they're better than me. I can't control the way others think about me. All I can be is me. All I can do is seek, ask questions and grow closer to the Lord as much as possible.

Sometimes talking to people is like dancing on thin ice. At any time, I may offend someone or give them the wrong impression, and like the ice, I crash into the cold sea and the conversation ends. Thus, leaving me and my *mission unaccomplished.* It's difficult to walk a life devoted to Jesus Christ, especially when everyone knows your past and can't seem to let you get past it. Yet to quit walking along this path, the path of following Jesus, is something I cannot do. Greenday may have a hit song claiming, “I walk alone,” but as for me...I walk with God.

The road can be lonely at times, but if you are faithful to God, if your heart, your mind, body, and soul are in pursuit of God, the road is a golden street of possibilities. The options are endless, for anything is possible with God. We must focus on our faith and how to keep it, especially as trials, temptations, and evil constantly surround us.

It's usually my big fat mouth that gets me into trouble...

MATHEW 15:11 Not that which goeth into the mouth defileth a man; but that which cometh out of the mouth, this defileth a man.

Hey, that's a lesson for me.

MATHEW 15:12-14 Then came his disciples, and said unto him, Knowest thou that the Pharisees, were offended, after they heard this saying?

But he answered and said, **Every plant, which my heavenly Father hath not planted, shall be rooted up.**

Let them alone: they be blind leaders of the blind. And if the blind lead the blind, both shall fall into the ditch.

Have you ever been offended by something that was written in the Bible? I have. Does it mean that the Bible is wrong? Or am I wrong? It is true that a very weak argument could be made to suggest that the Bible is contradictory. As Jesus came to fulfill the prophecies of the Old Testament, he also came to bring the New Testament to us. Whereas in the Old Testament offerings of sacrifice were made, in the New Testament, the ultimate sacrifice was made for all of our sins.

MATHEW 10:38-39 And he that taketh not his cross, and followeth after me, is not worthy of me. He that findeth his life shall lose it: and he that loseth his life for my sake shall find it.

I must "lose" the life that I think I want...and "find" the life that God has set for me. Easier said than done, but at least now I have an unselfish goal to strive for.

Looking Up To Heaven

It's easy to get wrapped up in my own world, to live a selfish and prideful life. It's more difficult to care about others – and actually put in the effort to try and help them. I don't believe in tough love, unless it is the love of God working to show me something, teach me a lesson or educate me spiritually, mentally, and physically. As we have sat in a classroom, looking up to the teacher, I sit here at my desk, looking up to Heaven – hoping to catch a glimpse of the creator through the stars at night and the cloudy blue sky during the day.

When I think about false flag events, I look up at Heaven, in search for answers. Before I do any research or writings on this subject, I pray that God has led me on this path for a reason. If I am doing this out of some selfish desire to get 'known' or 'famous,' then in the end, all of my life's journey will be for...***nothing.***

"One word, Nothing!"

CHAPTER TWO
TRUE MEANING OF CHRISTMAS

As a child I remember the Christmas season as one of the happiest times of the year. Everyone seemed to be in a better mood around this time. The air smelled fresher. The smiles stretched across peoples faces a bit more. Holiday joy was in the air. It seemed to me that every, "Merry Christmas," was met with, "And a Merry Christmas to you to sir." At this age, on Christmas day, I was certain of two things. Jesus Christ was born and Santa was coming to bring me presents. I thought that the reason why Santa brought presents to children was to celebrate the birth of Jesus Christ. After all, the old white bearded man was named Saint Nick. I naturally assumed he was a saint sent by God to bring presents to the world.

At that time, if I weighed Santa against Jesus Christ on a scale, it would always tip in favor of Santa. He brought presents. The other guy just had a birthday. Besides, I wanted presents! I wanted every Star Wars toy, every G.I. Joe action figure, every Rambo action figure and all the newest WWF wrestlers (especially the Ultimate Warrior). I was a greedy child.

Back then it seemed like it took forever for Christmas to come. Christmas morning would be a great day for me. I'd slowly open up every present. First we'd start with the stockings. Stocking stuffers are still a big part of our family Christmases. Being raised in a split family, I was guaranteed to have two Christmases every year. I thought that was the coolest thing in the world. What kid could say they had double the gifts on Christmas morning? It was great.

That is, until I learned about Easter and the meaning of it. That was a bit depressing. I read about and watched movies of Jesus being tormented, mocked, and murdered by people he loved. People just like you and I. That was when I began to understand the true meaning of Easter. My Grandma London had purchased some cartoons about the Bible when my little brother A.J. was a few years old.

He and I would watch the cartoons together. Well, the TV was on, but I don't know how interested A.J. was in them. I was very interested, as I had just had an awakening about Jesus Christ at that time; I was about 14 years old. I was in juvenile hall when the power of God struck me like a bolt of lightning. I prayed to be set free from that horrible place and about ten seconds later, I was free. To this day, I can't stand being in a locked room for very long. I constantly mark where the exits are at every restaurant, church, event, wedding, family function, or strangers house I go to. I make sure I have an exit that I can freely walk out of.

So watching a cartoon about how Jesus was born was fun for me. I never really heard Grandma London's views on spirituality, but I assume she believed in God and wanted A.J. to know God as well. She bought the entire 20 VHS collection, which I thought was pretty cool. It's a great way to get children excited about scripture. I think A.J. was too young to understand what was really going on in the cartoons, but I understood them. Of course, I was about 14 at the time, so I should have understood them anyway.

Grandma London single-handedly saved my family and I will never forget that. I would be foolish to think that her good deeds did not come from God. After she died, our phone would ring and ring...when I picked it up, there would be strange sounds at the other end, like using dial-up on your computer to connect to the Internet. It happened for like two days straight. It could have been prank calls, but I always thought it was Grandma London, trying to reach us. I have a strange feeling that she is still with us and will be watching over the boys until the end.

Man, I got off track for a minute...anyways, back to the Christmas story.

"700 years before the birth of Christ, it was as good as done. God made one of the many precious promises He will then keep." – **Pastor Scott Mueller**, East Hills Community Church

ISAIAH 9:6 For to us a child is born, to us a son is given, and the government will be on his shoulders. And he will be called Wonderful Counselor, Mighty God, Everlasting Father, Prince of Peace.

This is the true meaning of Christmas. The birth of our savior is the greatest gift that the world has ever known. For through this gift, salvation is made possible. Through salvation, I can get to Heaven. In Heaven, I can finally do what I've been waiting to do for my whole life, which is to touch the hand of God.

It was only when I learned that Santa Claus wasn't real that I began to understand the true meaning of Christmas. In the third grade, some kid in my class blurted out, "There is no Santa Claus!"

Those words stung me like a taser shot to the kidney. I searched for a flaw in that sentence. I asked my parents, who assured me Santa was real. Yet the more I thought about it, the more doubts I had about this. I never saw Santa, just the cookies and milk he would supposedly snack on after coming down our chimney. The only place I did see Santa was at the mall. It never occurred to me, "How can Santa be at Bayfair Mall and at Southland Mall at the same time?"

Some kid in my class had shattered my crystal image of Christmas. I asked my parents about these mall Santas. To which they replied, "Those are Santa's helpers."

Helpers? More like accomplices! I was a clueless third grader who never thought my parents would lie to me. My Grandma Fernandez would refer to it as a white lie, meaning it was a small lie that didn't hurt anybody. Those words gave me comfort. All of a sudden, that taser to my kidney vanished.

Still, as tradition would have it, I continued this white lie with my four younger siblings. More so with my two brothers A.J. and John. Anna and Sarah were forced to grow up too fast and they soon realized that Santa was a joke. Yet we kept up the lie, year after year until my little brothers figured out that Santa was fake.

The Satan in Santa Claus

People may think I'm making too much out of nothing when I think of the connection between Santa Claus and Satan. Yet five letters S-A-N-T-A can be switched around to spell, 'Satan.' This led me to wonder, "Is Santa Claus being used as a distraction to divert people away from the true meaning of Christmas? Did the Christmas tree come from Pagans? If it did, then why do many Christians, including myself, buy an overpriced tree every year? What does this have to do with the celebration of our Lord's birthday?

ReligiousTolerance.org states:

Apparently, in Jeremiah's time the "heathen" would cut down trees, carve or decorate them in the form of a God or Goddess, and overlay it with precious metals. Some Christians feel that this Pagan practice was similar enough to our present use of Christmas trees that

this passage from Jeremiah can be used to condemn both:

JERIMIAH 10:2-4 Thus saith the LORD, Learn not the way of the heathen, and be not dismayed at the signs of heaven; for the heathen are dismayed at them. For the customs of the people are vain: for one cutteth a tree out of the forest, the work of the hands of the workman, with the axe. They deck it with silver and with gold; they fasten it with nails and with hammers, that it move not.

Of course, these were not really Christmas trees, because Jesus was not born until centuries later, and the use of Christmas trees was not introduced for many centuries after his birth.

If people are focused on getting and giving presents, then what happens to the real focus we should have on this day? We should be celebrating the birth of our savior, more so than we celebrate giving gifts to others and receiving them ourselves. The true meaning of Christmas will never be changed, yet in our busy lives sometimes we need to be reminded of what Christmas is all about. It is about Jesus Christ. So let's remember that Santa is fake and The Christ is real. The tree is irrelevant, the meaning of Christmas is priceless.

"I write the checks when I get my bills and put a stamp on them and next to the stamp I write a little date. I don't mail it yet, it's not time, but I know it will be done. Does it seem to you that sometimes God does like I do with my bills? Sometimes I wish God would just put it in the mail...yesterday, but it's as good as mailed to Him. I have found that what I do while I am waiting for His promise may be even more important than what I do when He comes through for me." – **Pastor Scott Mueller**, East Hills Community Church

Merry Christmas. Happy Easter.

CHAPTER THREE
PURE RELIGION

If it is not the Bible, then what is it?

JAMES 1:27 Pure religion and undefiled before God and the Father is this, To visit the fatherless and widows in their affliction, and to keep himself unspotted from the world.

Spirituality has led me down a road that I didn't know existed. In the strangest of events, God has changed my life. Not too long ago, I thought I knew how to get to Heaven, how to be a good Christian and thought I had figured out ***all I needed to know*** about the meaning of life. As I grow in my spirituality, I am changing. My spirituality is the key to ***freeing*** my soul. To embrace my spirituality, I have tried to humble myself before God. I am trying to realize that I do not have the answers that I am searching for – nor will I find them by myself. I need God. I truly need God in my life in order to do this. For me to grow as a Christian, whether I believe in organized religion or not, I must learn – I must study the Bible as much as I can. What is the source of our Christianity? What is the source of our spirituality? If it is not the Bible, then what is it?

The Bible may be difficult for people like me to fully comprehend, but there are things inside that complicated book that I can comprehend and use in my life everyday. The lessons and history that are inside the Bible are the source to what we call spirituality or Christianity. What James 1:27 says to ***me*** is that pure religion is not about denominations, it's about helping others, "*the fatherless and the widows in their afflictions*." If we are Christians but are not reading and studying the Bible, how easy is it to fall off track? If we search for answers to life by looking outside of the Bible, what answers will we find? In order to logically disagree with the Bible, isn't it better to *understand* why you disagree? Or is it wise to simply disagree and move on...without doing the research? My spirituality is constantly being tested. My flesh lives with everlasting temptation, *for thy flesh is sinful.* Judging people for their faults has nothing to do with Christianity, helping others through these times has everything to do with Christianity. Some of the nicest people I have met are Christians, yet they are people just like you and I. They might fall down, just as we all do. It's a lot easier to pick yourself up with a little helping hand. That is how God works. Through people, God is working, fulfilling the prophecy of Judgment Day, better known as the end of time.

If it sounds crazy, it may be because you haven't studied the Bible. If you've never read or heard of the word of God, then perhaps it is crazy from that point of view. Given free will, every person is free to do *nothing* with their life and free to do *something*. Christianity is a life long progression, so it's unfair of me to say who is a Christian and who is not. Yet I catch myself doing this (bad Greg!). It is fair to say that only God knows who is truly a Christian and only God can get you to Heaven. With God by your side, your journey becomes clear. The Lord is always just a book, a prayer, or a thought away. However you choose to communicate with God, just make sure that you ***are*** communicating with God.

I'm tired of feeling embarrassed about talking to people about God – I am tired of worrying about whether I am going to offend someone because I choose to talk about God. But if I'm going to try to encourage others to read the Bible, I'd better be reading it too. Spread the Bible, not your interpretation of it. Let the word of God, the Bible, speak for itself. The word of God is speaking to us, not only in the Bible, but in the streets, in people, in actions – but if that is true, then how much more powerfully is the Bible speaking to us? How much more clearly does the Bible speak compared to any other way God may speak to you? Only you can answer this, as it relates to your own life. If God can speak to you through any means, anywhere, time, or place, then just imagine how he speaks to you directly from the Bible.

It is a powerful tool that God has given to us. So what shall we do with it, especially when we have a tough time understanding the 'meaning' of the Bible? That's where prayer comes in handy. I truly believe that God knows ***every*** prayer that I have ever said or thought.

"What do you base that belief on?"

"Faith."

"Why do you believe in an all powerful being, who controls our lives?"

"The word of God is so powerful, you can feel it. Read it and learn the way to salvation. I must believe that I am going to Heaven. I must have faith." Yet even faith should be *based* on something more than a hypothetical guess. Faith is not science, but science has helped strengthen my faith. Just as faith has helped strengthen scientists in their quest to prove God does not exist, I strengthen my faith to prove there is a God, Jesus Christ, and he is a loving God above all else. The faithless fall into a pit of despair – anger may drive them to say irrational things.

Yet when all else fails you in life, God will not – as long as you have faith and try to develop a relationship with God. If you ignore God, a lot of the time, you are on your own. Even then, when you pray to God, you do so because you hope he will listen and answer your prayers. Your hope is your faith, and this proves that you do believe in God. Even if you keep it to yourself, God knows your heart, your mind, your body, and your soul.

CHAPTER FOUR
GOD WILL SAVE US

MATHEW 27:42-43 He saved others; himself he cannot save. If he be the king of Israel, let him now come down from the cross, and we will believe him. He trusted in God; let him deliver him now, if he will have him: for he said, I am the Son of God.

We have all been condemned sometime in our life. He could have walked away from the cross but he didn't. Instead, he sacrificed himself and changed everything – he forgave us for our sins and gave us physical proof by dying as a human, on the cross. You too, can walk away from the Bible, from Christianity, or Jesus...but why would you want to? I wonder if that's what Jesus was thinking.

LUKE 23:37...If thou be the king of the Jews, save thyself.

What seemed logical to these earthly beings, may have been backwards in the spiritual realm. He was saving us all by not walking away from the cross. He did not abandon us then, why would he abandon us now? God does not abandon his people, it is usually the other way around. If you're not learning about God, practicing his word, or being a good human being, perhaps you have abandoned God? Perhaps...but that's for you to decide.

As Jesus was about to 'give up the ghost,' with one criminal to the left, and one to the right, it became clear to me that ***anyone and everyone at anytime in their life can get the call to Heaven. We have to have faith that we can all get to Heaven if we believe in Christ!*** This next scripture taught me that. Although some may see this as my interpretation of the Bible and say I'm wrong...I'm cool with that.

LUKE 23:39-43 And one of the malefactors which were hanged railed on him, saying, If thou be Christ, save thyself and us. But the other answering rebuked him, saying, 'Dost not thou fear God, seeing thou art in the same condemnation? And we indeed justly; for we receive the due reward of our deeds: but this man hath done nothing amiss.' And he said unto Jesus, 'Lord, remember me when thou comest into thy kingdom.'

And Jesus said unto him, **Verily I say unto thee, Today shalt thou be with me in paradise.**

The man to whom Jesus said, "Today shalt thou be with me in paradise," was just like you and I, a thief! We are all guilty of something. Yet even as this man died, he had faith that Jesus was the Christ. Through his faith, he was saved. He obviously didn't have the New Testament like I do today and yes, he saw the physical presence of Jesus; but so did many others, including his own family, yet they did not believe...but the thief did.

This is a valuable lesson I use in my life. More so, Jesus did not condemn others who mocked him. Instead Jesus simply said, "Father forgive them; for they know not what they do." Jesus knows we are going to screw up. In the eyes of God, what is time? God knows the beginning, the middle, and the end of time. Why do we humans try to copy ***that***? Isn't our faith enough?

LUKE 24:7 The son of man must be delivered into the hands of sinful men, and be crucified, and the third day rise again.

With the prophecy fulfilled, Jesus 'gave up the ghost' only to rise from the grave three days later. Hard to believe? Not with faith, education, and an open mind. The body of Jesus was put in a clean, unused grave, "a sepulchre (tomb or burial chamber) that was hewn in stone, wherein never man before was laid."

LUKE 23:52-53 This man went unto Pilate, and begged the body of Jesus. And he took it down and wrapped it in linen, and laid it in a sepulchre that was hewn in stone, wherein never man before was laid.

MATHEW 27:59-60 And when Joseph had taken the body, he wrapped it in a clean linen cloth, And laid it in his own new tomb, which he had hewn out in the rock: and he rolled a great stone to the door of the sepulchre, and departed.

Where'd All Those Saints Come From?

MATHEW 27:50-53 Jesus, when he had cried again with a loud voice, yielded up the ghost. And, behold, the veil of the temple was rent in twain from the top to the bottom; and the earth did quake, and the rocks rent; And the graves were opened; and many bodies of the saints which slept arose, and came out of the graves after his resurrection, and went into the holy city, and appeared unto many.

This still has me baffled...but guess what...I have some great sources for getting some knowledge on this subject and I intend to use them. Were these saints in Hades? Were they walking zombies going into church? Did they have consciousness? Why are they mentioned in only one verse (that I could find)? Is this fact insignificant in the bigger picture? Does this show that seeing is believing for us humans? Is this a question I should be dwelling on?

I can answer the last question. The answer is, "No." *But why?* I ask myself. There are so many questions that I have about the Bible. My friend German has read the Bible many times. He explained to me that you can read a verse a thousand times and not understand it. Then you read that same verse years later and it makes sense. I asked a speaker at our church about this in an email. Here's the response I got from Chuck Austin:

Hi! Yes, I've been speaking at East Hills...You ask some very good questions. Suffice it to say that the resurrection of Jesus had a profound effect and impact on not only the living but the dead.

Where were these saints? That's a good question and I'm not sure anyone has the answer to that. Your observation on why more was not written about them is a good one. But remember the Gospel writers had specific reasons on why they wrote --- Matthew shows a lot of Old Testament fulfillment in Jesus. He probably figured that the mention of them was enough --- since so many had seen them personally. Plus the Gospel was about Jesus and what God did in triumphing over death.

It was Jesus in John 14:1-6 who said He was coming to get people and take them back to where He was. Until that time, those who trusted in God did exactly that --- they trusted in God. But there wasn't much for them beyond that except the promise of the Messiah. Once Jesus came, everything changed.

I hope that helps. If I wasn't clear or you have other questions, don't hesitate to let me know!!

~~Chuck

So if you read the Bible and do not understand it, don't get too discouraged. It happens to us all. My father-in-law has been reading the Bible for almost as long as I've been alive and he still doesn't understand everything in it. How much harder will it be for someone like me?

"Tis a lesson you should heed, Try, try again. If at first you don't succeed, Try, try again." - **Thomas H. Palmer** (1782 – 1861)

I have failed to understand certain things in the Bible...so guess what I am going to do? Sometimes, it's not about being right or wrong, it's about learning what is right and what is wrong. To do that, you have to seek, you have to look. Where better to look than to Heaven?

REVELATIONS 22:18-19 For I testify unto every man that heareth the words of the prophecy of this book, If any man shall add unto these things, God shall add unto him the plagues that are written in this book:

And if any man shall take away from the words of the book of this prophecy, God shall take away his part out of the book of life, and out of the holy city, and from the things which are written in this book.

CHAPTER FIVE
WHAT IS TRUTH?

"It takes two to speak the truth - one to speak and another to hear." – **Thoreau**

What is truth?

JOHN 8:31 Then said Jesus to those Jews which believed on him, **If ye continue in my word, then are ye my disciples indeed; And ye shall know the truth, and the truth shall make you free.**

1 JOHN 1:5-7 ...God is light, and in him is no darkness at all.
If we say that we have fellowship with him, and walk in darkness, we lie, and do not the truth: But if we walk in the light, as he is in the light, we have fellowship one with another, and the blood of Jesus Christ his Son cleanseth us from all sin.

Sometimes the truth is right in front of our face and we just need someone to open our eyes to things we should already know about.

"They spent a hundred million dollars to discover Bill Clinton's cheated on Hillary, when on 9-11 they only allocated four million to find out who killed 3,000 people." – **Gov. Jesse Ventura** (Larry King, July 2009)

Living a truthful life does not come without flaws, failures, and sacrifices. It's easy to point out the faults of my neighbors. It's more difficult to look myself in the mirror and confess my own faults before God. Who is without fault? Whose sins outweigh my own? What will I do when I see darkness all around me? Who can I turn to? Where will I find truth in the shadows of the world? What is truth? What does God ask of his people?

MATHEW 28:19-20 Go ye therefore, and teach all nations, baptizing them in the name of the Father, and of the Son, and of the

Holy Ghost: Teaching them to observe all things whatsoever I have commanded you: and, lo, I am with you always, even unto the end of the world. Amen.

A person's soul, or what Whitney Houston calls her dignity, cannot be taken away or touched by any other, except God. The truth is in our soul. We just have to open our hearts, our minds, and realize that we may not know truth yet...though we continually seek it.

JOHN 18:33-40 Pilate then went back inside the palace, summoned Jesus and asked him, "Are you the king of the Jews?"

"**Is that your own idea,**" Jesus asked, "**or did others talk to you about me?**"

"Am I a Jew?" Pilate replied. "It was your people and your chief priests who handed you over to me. What is it you have done?"

Jesus said, "**My kingdom is not of this world. If it were, my servants would fight to prevent my arrest by the Jews. But now my kingdom is from another place.**"

"You are a king, then!" said Pilate.

Jesus answered, "**You are right in saying I am a king. In fact, for this reason I was born, and for this I came into the world, to testify to the truth. Everyone on the side of truth listens to me.**"

"What is truth?" Pilate asked.

With this he went out again to the Jews and said, "I find no basis for a charge against him. But it is your custom for me to release to you one prisoner at the time of the Passover. Do you want me to release 'the king of the Jews'?"

They shouted back, "No, not him! Give us Barabbas!" Now Barabbas had taken part in a rebellion.

As I seek truth, I realize how little I know about it. Just as when I began to take the Bible seriously, I understood that I had so much learning to do. To catch a spec of wisdom is not easy, but it is possible with the proper guidance. Where else would we look to but to Heaven? The Bible is like our blue print, our spine, our 'core' to seeking truth. To understand truth, first I must seek it. If I think I have found it, I probably haven't. Once I stop seeking, the truth becomes blinded by my own thoughts. It's as if truth is continually moving, rotating like an axis around the world. For if truth was once found only in the Old Testament, did truth change when the

New Testament was created? What is truth?

Useless Categories

Why do we put ourselves into meaningless categories? Of course every being is different, that goes without saying. But when we categorize ourselves, it makes it easier for someone else to catalog what type of people we are. It is usually done for simplicity, but is it really necessary? Should we catalog people like we do cattle? Well, some people in this world may see *you* as cattle. How does that sound to you? How does it make you feel, knowing that someone may be controlling what goes on in your life, without you ever realizing it?

I ask myself, "*How does that make you feel Mr. Pride?*"

My response is, "*not too good.*"

That is where deception comes in. If you are deceived into believing you are in full control of your life, it may be difficult for you to grow spiritually. I say that because you may be doing what you think you should, without referring to the Bible for the answers. How can you grow if you're not listening to the Bible? It's like the blind leading the blind. If you don't think you need God in your life, or if you think that the Bible is *not that important*, it's like having a beautiful seed with no fertilizer or water. If you do not grow, there's a good chance you remain ignorant and may become "set in your ways."

Doesn't Jesus want us to grow? To serve is to grow, because you are thinking of others, rather than just yourself. You grow by helping others grow. You are helping others grow so that you too may grow. The only truth I am certain of is that I am being deceived every day by various sources, people, institutions and religions. In the end, it's how I deal with them that matters to me. This is part of my growth; to learn, to discover, to seek, and to share. I know Jesus forgives, because it's in the Bible. What type of Christian is not seeking answers in the Bible? In my opinion, it's the selfish type. Am I wrong? Perhaps...but I can live with that. I have seen miracles that opened doors to fresh new life, when all hope seemed gone. I have seen the answers to my prayers come in ways that I could never have imagined. I have had things in my life *pass my way* that have changed me forever. It is by the grace of God that all this is possible.

MATHEW 15:11 Not that which goeth into the mouth defileth a man; but that which cometh out of the mouth, this defileth a man.

In my opinion, people who blame God for their own problems, or for the problems of the world, do not yet understand God. Here's the deceptive part in that statement – my words can be interpreted that I know *who knows God* and *who doesn't*. That is simply not the truth. Only God knows that for sure. The devil sows seeds of deceitfulness. Shall we let him plant his seeds in our head?

Get away from me Satan.

Much Ado About Something

With God by my side, I learn *something* every day, even when I don't want to. People really think that once we have finished this cause for truth that we will just find another task to latch onto. That is what I call 'writing me off,' and it happens to me all the time. It's easier to write me off than to listen and possibly get involved in a cause that is bigger than any one person. Those people come to that conclusion willingly. Just as I have come to my conclusion willingly. I don't need to prove that I am right. I am searching for the truth. What I know is that we don't know what happened on September 11th. We don't know why WTC Building 7 fell down the same way as WTC Towers One and Two. What we know is what we don't know, get it?

So we have a lot of work to do. It's one thing to be a pacifist in this info-war; it's another thing to be an accomplice to the real criminals and murderers of 9-11-2001. Anyone trying to suppress or put down the 9-11 truth movement can be considered an accomplice, if you want. More often than not, I tend to agree with that statement. So we have even more work to do. Since this world is temporary, why should I focus on worldly and materialistic things? It doesn't mean that I am attacking anyone who does these things either.

I like worldly things too. But I understand that it's wrong and doesn't really help me grow spiritually, unless I can apply my spiritual journey to this obsession I have with worldly things, such as writing and making music. If I can use these two things to further my spiritual growth, then why shouldn't I? What I do now and until the end of my life is not only for me and you, but for our children and their children's children. We must consider the future of humanity and the future of our spiritual growth.

MARK 9:42 And whosoever shall offend one of these little ones that believe in me, it is better for him that a millstone were hanged about his neck, and he were cast into the sea.

Ouch. That's gotta hurt. That could be me. That could be you. That could be any of us! I think that's why repentance is so important. We will have failures in life. It's how we deal with our failures that matter in the end. We will be measured by our entire life's works, not one aspect of it. This is also why forgiveness is so important. If you cannot forgive another, why should you expect God to forgive you?

1 JOHN 1:8-10 If we say that we have no sin, we deceive ourselves, and the truth is not in us. If we confess our sins, he is faithful and just to forgive us our sins, and to cleanse us from all unrighteousness. If we say that we have not sinned, we make him a liar, and his word is not in us.

We Are All Sinners

What are we doing to fight the sinful temptations that we face every day? How can we stand toe to toe with an evil that does not rest, never sleeps, and is always present? With humans, this is impossible...but with God all things are possible.

MATHEW 4:19 Follow me, and I will make you fishers of men.
God has commanded us to spread the word.

MARK 6:4 ...A prophet is not without honor, but in his own country, and among his own kin, and in his own house.

Perhaps this is why the relatives and the people who knew Jesus as a boy had a difficult time believing he was the son of God – yet over 3,000 strangers at a time were quick to have faith in him.

MARK 6:3 Is not this the carpenter, the son of Mary, the brother of James, and Joses, and of Juda, and Simon? And are not his sisters here with us? And they were offended at him.

MARK 6:6 And he marvelled because of their unbelief. And he went round about the villages, teaching.

Still, Jesus sent his twelve disciples "*by two and two; and gave them power over unclean spirits*." It is written that because of the lack of faith in his own home town, *"he could do no mighty work, save that he laid his hands upon a few sick folk, and healed them.*"

MARK 9:31 The son of man is delivered into the hands of men, and they shall kill him; and after that he is killed, he shall rise the third day.

The ultimate sacrifice was made when Jesus died on the cross for our sins. Let us never forget the true meaning of Easter. As a matter of fact let us never forget the true meaning of Christmas. Sorry kids, there is no Santa Claus. However, there is, has been, and always will be God, Jesus Christ and the Holy Spirit. Go with God my friends.

CHAPTER SIX
THE TRUTH IS GOD

LUKE 23:26-47 When they led Him away, they seized a man, Simon of Cyrene, coming in from the country, and placed on him the cross to carry behind Jesus. And following Him was a large crowd of the people, and of women who were mourning and lamenting Him.

But Jesus turning to them said, "**Daughters of Jerusalem, stop weeping for me, but weep for yourselves and for your children. For behold, the days are coming when they will say, 'Blessed are the barren, and the wombs that never bore, and the breasts that never nursed.' Then they will begin to say to the mountains, 'Fall on us,' and to the hills, 'Cover us.' For if they do these things when the tree is green, what will happen when it is dry?"**

Two others also, who were criminals, were being led away to be put to death with Him. When they came to the place called The Skull, there they crucified Him and the criminals, one on the right and the other on the left.

But Jesus was saying, **"Father, forgive them; for they do not know what they are doing."** And they cast lots, dividing up His garments among themselves. And the people stood by, looking on.

And even the rulers were sneering at Him, saying, "He saved others; let Him save Himself if this is the Christ of God, His Chosen One."

The soldiers also mocked Him, coming up to Him, offering Him sour wine, and saying, "If You are the King of the Jews, save yourself!" Now there was also an inscription above Him, "THIS IS THE KING OF THE JEWS."

One of the criminals who were hanged there was hurling abuse at Him, saying, "Are You not the Christ? Save yourself and us!"

But the other answered, and rebuking him said, "Do you not even fear God, since you are under the same sentence of condemnation? And we indeed are suffering justly, for we are receiving what we deserve for our deeds; but this man has done nothing wrong." And he was saying, "Jesus, remember me when You come in Your kingdom!"

And He said to him, "**Truly I say to you, today you shall be with**

Me in Paradise." It was now about the sixth hour, and darkness fell over the whole land until the ninth hour, because the sun was obscured; and the veil of the temple was torn in two.

And Jesus, crying out with a loud voice, said, **"Father, into Your hands I commit My spirit."** Having said this, He breathed His last.

Now when the centurion saw what had happened, he began praising God, saying, "Certainly this man was innocent."

Faith…faith cometh by hearing and hearing by the Lord. Truth is what I have set out to find. I now understand why people abandon the search for truth. You can speculate on what truth is, but you will only know for sure once you have died. If you believe you have found truth, then what is there left to search for? "What is truth," Pilate asked Jesus. Even the governors of the Roman Empire searched for some truths in their day. From the early stages of consciousness, we begin this search. What we find along the way helps us try to answer this question. What is the meaning of life? How does it relate to me? Why am I here?

Only God knows for sure. To seek out these answers, we must turn to the Bible. All we need to know is right there in black and white print. Everything else, in my opinion, is secondary. If we are not actively reading the Bible (myself included) then how much effort are we putting into seeking God? I believe in Jesus Christ. I read and question the Bible, for better or for worse. I don't have to agree with everything in the Bible to know it is ***truth***. Just because I don't agree with some passages does not mean that the passages are wrong. It means that *I* am wrong.

In a deeper sense it may mean that God has not opened up my eyes to these truths, yet. I must continue to search for truth, continue to follow Jesus and continue to pray. Doing these three things, I believe I will find what I am searching for. It is hard to put my selfish desires ahead of God's will, especially when following God's will seems so simple at times. Temptation can get the best of me, but I'm working on that. As long as God is with me, I know I'll be alright. How do I know if God is with me?

Philippians 3:7-14 But whatever was to my profit I now consider loss for the sake of Christ. What is more, I consider everything a loss compared to the surpassing greatness of knowing Christ Jesus my Lord, for whose sake I have lost all things. I consider them rubbish, that I may gain Christ and be found in him, not having a righteousness of my own that comes from the law, but that which is through faith in Christ—the righteousness that comes from God and is by faith. I want to know Christ and the power of his resurrection and the fellowship of sharing in his sufferings, becoming like him in his death, and so, somehow, to attain to the resurrection from the dead. Not that I have already obtained all this, or have already been made perfect, but I press on to take hold of that for which Christ Jesus took hold of me. Brothers, I do not consider myself yet to have taken hold of it. But one thing I do: Forgetting what is behind and straining toward what is ahead, I press on toward the goal to win the prize for which God has called me heavenward in Christ Jesus.

I believe. Faith. To have faith in something greater than you will set you free from the burdens of this world. When my life is not about 'me,' my life is easier. I could be self serving, self loathing, or selfless. Right now I am a little bit of all three. I am a work in progress. As long as I realize this, as long as I try to stay humble, I will eventually find truth…I will eventually see God.

ROMANS 9:1-5 I say the truth in Christ, I lie not, my conscience also bearing me witness in the Holy Ghost,

That I have great heaviness and continual sorrow in my heart. For I could wish that myself were accursed from Christ for my brethren, my kinsmen according to the flesh:

Who are Israelites; to whom pertaineth the adoption, and the glory, and the covenants, and the giving of the law, and the service of God, and the promises;

Whose are the fathers, and of whom as concerning the flesh Christ came, who is over all, God blessed for ever. Amen.

Ask yourself...what is truth? Then go out and seek it.

CHAPTER SEVEN
WHAT DO YOU WANT ME TO DO?

What has God called you to do? What does Jesus tell us to do? Spread the gospel and the news. He has risen! To look up at Heaven with humility and obedience to God is no easy task. Yet we are called upon to spread the word of God, to learn about salvation, and to be kind to each other. Through our actions, others will see what kind of people we are. There is truth in the theory that those who have God are not miserable. God takes care of those who obey his commands, have faith, and try to follow his teachings. God blesses those who help out others. God truly hears our prayers. Even if our prayers are not answered immediately, God does hear us. All we have to do is believe.

Faith requires patience. I learned this while watching the movie, "Willy Wonka and The Chocolate Factory." A young spoiled girl named Veruca shouts out to her father, "But I want it now!" Her pudgy father shakes his waddle as he answers, "As soon as we get home." Home is Heaven, where everything is waiting for us. Don't you want to go home some day? "But I want to go now!" Me too. For now, we must have patience. We must seek God with an open mind and an understanding heart. As Jesus showed compassion for us, we must show compassion for others.

Veruca learned this the hard way. After throwing a singing tantrum in front of Mr. Wonka's other guests, she is finally dumped into a shute where the golden eggs go, the bad eggs anyways. Her asking is what granted her what she thought she wanted, though it was not as golden as she would have hoped. Had she been patient, perhaps she might have gotten a good golden egg. Instead she ended up with *nothing*, worthless eggs that were thrown away on a routine basis. What a pity.

As I sat and watched this movie, and her destruction, I said to myself, "whoa, that's not how I want to be." In todays TV programs, the valuable lessons get lost in the vanity of getting what you want. Sometimes what you think you want is not what God wants for you. How do you know? Only time will tell. To wait for the right timing takes patience. Patience is not an easy thing to practice, but it can be done. Do we seek what we want or what God wants from us? Skimming through my Bible one day, I noticed there were writings and notes that my brother had made while reading it. He circled some passages that might have been powerful to him. He underlined certain scriptures that perhaps he felt were what he'd come back to later. On the top of one page he wrote, "What do you want me to do God?"

I was awestruck. Wow, this question was so important to him that he had to write it down in the Bible. I asked myself the same question. That was over ten years ago. I am beginning to understand what God wants me to do. Just as the 12 disciples were witnesses of Jesus Christ and spread his teachings, I should try to do the same to the best of my ability.

ACTS 1:8 You shall receive power when the Holy Spirit has come upon you; and you shall be witnesses to Me...to the end of the earth.

What does God want us to do here on earth?

Colossians 3:12-17 Since God chose you to be the holy people whom he loves, you must clothe yourselves with tenderhearted mercy, kindness, humility, gentleness, and patience. You must make allowance for each other's faults and forgive the person who offends you. Remember, the Lord forgave you, so you must forgive others. And the most important piece of clothing you must wear is love. Love is what binds us all together in perfect harmony. And let the peace that comes from Christ rule in your hearts. For as members of one body you are all called to live in peace. And always be thankful. Let the words of Christ, in all their richness, live in your hearts and make you wise. Use his words to teach and counsel each other. Sing psalms and hymns and spiritual songs to God with thankful hearts. And whatever you do or say, let it be as a representative of the Lord Jesus, all the while giving thanks through him to God the Father.

CHAPTER EIGHT
MOLECH EXPOSED

"I've gotta talk to you about that someday," said my Pastor, Scott Mueller. That was an accomplishment for me. Whether he thought it was true or not, he seemed like he was interested in the connection between Molech and our political leaders. Maybe he was humoring me or being polite, but as I told him, researching this connection brought me closer to God than I ever thought possible. That's also when I began to work at a Christian radio station, so I'm sure that had something to do with it too. Alex Jones played a pivotal role in my spirituality. His brave venture to expose these elitists worshiping Molech (the owl God to whom parents would sacrifice their children to) would forever change my life. At the time, I was researching 9/11 conspiracy theories, thanks to my brother Ilya Petushkov. Never did I imagine that God was *reeling me into his net*. I was the fish in the water and God was pulling me out, in order to help me grow.

JOHN 21:5-6 Then Jesus saith unto them, **Children, have ye any meat?** They answered him, No. And he said unto them, **Cast the net on the right side of the ship, and ye shall find**. They cast therefore, and now they were not able to draw it for the multitude of fishes.

Alex broke into the Bohemian Grove complex in Marin County, near Monte Rio. His footage set a fire storm under the feet of the world elite. He had exposed what others called a *theory*, that satanic worship was taking place at this 'all male retreat,' proving it was factual. Thank God for the creation of cameras!

LEVITICUS 20:4-5 If the people of the community close their eyes when that man gives one of his children to Molech and they fail to put him to death, I will set my face against that man and his family and will cut off from their people both him and all who follow him in prostituting themselves to Molech.

Some of our world leaders are meeting at the Bohemian Grove club to do just that. They openly defy the God they tell the people they praise. Is this the definition of blasphemy? People voted for certain government officials because they thought they were Christians. These people have been known to frequent the Bohemian Grove. Richard Nixon stated on record his disgust for the 'queer' behavior taking place at the Bohemian Grove. It is claimed that this was the place that the 'Manhattan Project' was created. I don't know.

“The Bohemian Grove -- which I attend, from time to time -- it is the most faggy goddamned thing you could ever imagine, with that San Francisco crowd. I can't shake hands with anybody from San Francisco.” – **Richard Nixon**

I do believe it's worth looking into what the Bohemian Grove is, what type of satanic rituals take place there, and if any elected government officials attend. I also think that any elected officials who have been to the Grove should be able to answer questions as to what they were doing there and why they were there? More so, why would they, as men of faith, support a place that openly had a 'fake' human sacrifice before a giant wooden owl?

DEUTERONOMY 12:31 You must not worship the Lord your God in their way, because in worshiping their Gods, they do all kinds of detestable things the Lord hates. They even burn their sons and daughters in the fire as sacrifices to their Gods.

Would you attend a 'club' like this if you knew they were doing rituals on the same property? Even if you had nothing to do with it, never went to the ritual (as I believe and hope a lot of people didn't) or wanted any part of it, why support this type of behavior? Why not disassociate yourself from that type of behavior? If business is done on the golf course, then I guess you have to go to the golf course to do your business too right? That's fine for golf and private business, but not for elected public officials. They answer to the people, not to any group or faction that is not part of the United States government. My journey began there. It will not end until I am gone from this earth; which I hope is a long time from now. When Jesus walked the earth, people wished only to touch the garment he was wearing, believing they would be healed if they did so. Their faith healed them, as Jesus would say many times in the Bible. The reoccurring theme in those scriptures is faith. Before we get back to the Molech exposure, let's be reminded about faith, as is written in John 20:25.

JOHN 20:25 The other disciples therefore said unto him, We have seen the Lord. But he said unto them, Except I shall see in his hands the print of the nails, and thrust my hand into his side, I will not believe. And after eight days again his disciples were within, and Thomas with them: then came Jesus, the doors being shut, and stood in the midst, and said, Peace be unto you. Then saith he to Thomas, Reach hither thy finger, and behold my hands: and reach hither thy hand and thrust it into my side: and be not faithless, but believing.

Even those who were there in the days of the Christ had trouble believing he was the son of God. They did not seem to understand, fully, what he was doing on earth and why things had to happen, such as his death.

JOHN 20:29 Jesus said unto him, Thomas, because thou hast seen me, thou hast believed: blessed are they that have not seen, and yet have believed.

Back to Molech. Sometimes seeing helps our belief. It helped me to see the ritual where these grown men sacrificed an effigy (a fake wooden baby) before Molech. It's bad enough that this is actually happening. It's worse to know that some of these people are, may know, or may be affiliated with, elected representatives and officials of the United States Government. That is where I have drawn the line.

JERIMIAH 7:30-31 The people of Israel have done evil in my eyes, declares the Lord...They have built the high places of Topeth in the Valley of Ben Hinnom to burn their sons and daughters in the fire-something I did not command, nor did it enter my mind.

It sounds like something you would only hear in a horror story. Yet it's real. As Alex Jones videotaped, there are people who are still 'playing' out fantasies of sacrificing humans to an owl god, whether fake or not. (There is no evidence, and I offer no speculation to suggest this ritual today is performed using a real human being.) It's bad enough to support an event where this takes place. It's worse to attend. For private citizens it may be different, but for elected officials they should have to make it public knowledge if they do attend an event at the Bohemian Grove in Northern California. Why? The people of The United States have the right to know if our elected officials are attending a satanic ritual.

PSALMS 106:37-38 They sacrificed their sons and their daughters to demons. They shed innocent blood, the blood of their sons and daughters, whom they sacrificed to the idols of Canaan, and the land was desecrated by their blood.

The devil tempts people with lustful gifts. The master of confusion will delve into your deepest darkest fantasies and use them against you. That's why it's important to know God. The closer you are to God, the further you will be from the devil.

ACTS 7:43 You also took along the tabernacle of Molech and the star of the God Rompha, the images which you made to worship. I also will remove you beyond Babylon.

Dark Secrets of the Bohemian Grove can be seen on the Internet for free. Watch as Alex Jones films his entrance, the sacrificial "Cremation of Care," and the Grove's giant owl, who bares the symbol of the false god Molech. You really have to see the footage to believe what happens at this all male summer retreat. The evidence is there in this video, which can be seen on You Tube as well. Will you take a moment to examine this evidence? It's a quick search away...

CHAPTER NINE
WORSHIP

In my opinion, a good pastor is a man who can walk into the world and know that he should not be tempted by the evils of this planet, a man who can be humble, though God has given him stature in the spiritual realm, with responsibilities not only to his family but to all of God's people. A good pastor must be seen as a regular person with faults and sins as we all have. A great pastor can take a blind man full of sin and help him see the Lord Jesus Christ. A great pastor takes this same man, though he may be late 9 times out of 10 to church, and helps this man wake up every Sunday wanting to go to church and learn about Christ and follow the Lord.

Thank you for helping my blind eyes see. Though we at the church do not *see* all the miracles and wonders that happen because of the glory of God, we have faith that God will continue to do so and bring pastors from Michigan to Africa, or to California to do the work of our Lord and Father in Heaven. If I didn't try to warn people, I'd feel guilty. Even though warning them may make me seem ‘crazy' in their world, in the real world, “Only God can judge me.” I once cared about impressions and it only brought me anxiety and anger. Maybe impression is the wrong word; I mix up impressions with assumptions. People assume if you are against Bush, you're for Obama. If you're a Christian, you should act in a stereo typical way. If you believe in conspiracy theories, you're a few screws loose. I watched the movie **Endgame** again last night. I had this gut feeling telling me to look into holding a screening of this movie at our church. I believe Endgame provides many questions and God provides the answers.

If I can articulate this in the right way, maybe I can accomplish this “new found” goal. The church is the key to beating the new world order. That is why they (those who are willingly supervised, or unwittingly manipulated by the devil) have infiltrated it since the early days of mankind. I got sick of people thinking they knew me, where I was, what I was doing and so forth. I found myself arguing to prove myself right and finally said, “Forget this.” If they really care about me and who I am, then they will accept me for who I am, even if their impression of me is totally fictional and full of assumptions that they can't back up.

One of my oldest best friends thinks I am at times 'crazy and extreme.' If that doesn't bother me, people at the church thinking the same thing is a minor obstacle. I wish I could get five minutes in front of the church to try and explain these things. You know what, I am going to pray about this and if it be God's will, it will happen. Before I try to preach to my church, I have a lot of learning and growing to do. This thought was reinforced when I read this passage in the Bible:

PROVERBS 3:7-8 Do not be wise in your own eyes; Fear the LORD and turn away from evil. It will be healing to your body and refreshment to your bones.

Reading this next passage, I have learned how important it is to be humble:

ISAIAH 57:15 The high and lofty one who inhabits eternity, the Holy One, says this: "I live in that high and holy place with those whose spirits are contrite and humble. I refresh the humble and give new courage to those with repentant hearts.

I know that one day, Jesus will return...

ACTS 3:20...wonderful times of refreshment will come from the presence of the Lord, and he will send Jesus your Messiah to you again.

I have felt the power of love in helping others. The feeling is indescribable. There is no greater feeling than that which I feel when helping others.

PROVERBS 11:25 The generous prosper and are satisfied; those who refresh others will themselves be refreshed.

The more I read the Bible, the more I realize how weak-minded I am. I see how far I have to go to get to the promise land. I look up to the stars and wonder what Heaven is like. I wonder what the world will be like after Jesus Christ returns and Judgment Day is over. What then? I have this gnawing feeling that I am always going to be somewhere doing something...sometimes this feeling plagues me with anxiety. What is Heaven like? Why are we suffering here on earth? Why must this be? What's the point? What is God and who created God? I know that all good things come to those who wait, but it can be exhausting when you're asking the same questions you were asking thirty years ago. The unanswerable questions get my blood flowing and pierce my brainwaves.

"But I want the answers now!" I say to myself.

Where's my faith? Where's my trust that in good time, God will reveal these things to me? Sometimes I linger on my doubts longer than I should. Yet on Sunday morning, while I'm sitting in church, all I feel is calmness. I feel protected. I feel like I'm in my Father's arms. Nothing can hurt me then. Nothing can destroy my faith...nothing can tempt me to do the things I know I shouldn't do. For that brief hour and a half a week, I am truly looking up to Heaven – with all my faith. Many people have been my spiritual influences; including my family, strangers, my friends, TV and radio personalities and of course, Pastor Scott Mueller.

"Lord, wake me up this morning with renewed strength and resolve to hear your voice and walk with you and live for you. Revive me and refresh me today so that I can be useful and productive and prepared for whatever comes my way. I lay my plans, my weaknesses and failures, my gifts and talents at your feet and ask you to go with me now into my day, help me to recognize your provision of refreshment today. Lord help me to be a cup of refreshing cold water to another dry and thirsty person, in need of you today. In Jesus Name, Amen." – **Pastor Scott Mueller** (East Hills Community Church, 12000 Campus Drive, Oakland, CA 94619, 510.531.7100)

When life has you on the ropes, when all hope fades away, when the darkest hour is at hand...look up to Heaven, pray to the Lord, meditate on your thoughts, and most important of all, maintain your faith in Jesus. God is with you *even until the end of the world*. Never forget that. There is no problem too small or big that you can't run to God, crying with open arms. As a loving father will do, God will open his arms and embrace you. God loves you so much. Never forget this. Never let anyone tell you otherwise...no matter what you have done in your life. It is never too late to begin a relationship with God. It is never foolish to cry out to God.

God loves you! How awesome is our God? How awesome our God is!

CHAPTER TEN
FAITH TO HEAL

MATHEW 17:14-21 When they came to the crowd, a man approached Jesus and knelt before him. "Lord, have mercy on my son," he said. "He has seizures and is suffering greatly. He often falls into the fire or into the water. I brought him to your disciples, but they could not heal him.

"O unbelieving and perverse generation," Jesus replied, **"how long shall I stay with you? How long shall I put up with you? Bring the boy here to me."** Jesus rebuked the demon, and it came out of the boy, and he was healed from that moment.

Then the disciples came to Jesus in private and asked, "Why couldn't we drive it out?"

He replied, **"Because you have so little faith. I tell you the truth, if you have faith as small as a mustard seed, you can say to this mountain, 'Move from here to there' and it will move. Nothing will be impossible for you."**

In order to believe that the Bible is the *true* word, we must have faith. Our research of the Bible strengthens our faith. Reading the Bible gives us the answers to the questions we seek...*why are we here? What does God want me to do?*

The Lord is many things. In reading the Bible, I have found many scriptures where the Lord is merciful. The Lord is our teacher, so as students, we must pay attention to what is being said. Prayer is an essential tool that we should use every day.

MATHEW 9:36 But when he saw the multitudes, he was moved with compassion on them, because they fainted, and were scattered abroad, as sheep having no shepherd. Then saith he unto his disciples, The harvest truly is plenteous, but the labourers are few. Pray ye therefore the Lord of the harvest, that he will send forth labourers into his harvest.

That is us! We are the laborers. It's easier said than done. Yet God knows our works, from every time we help one another to any prayer we give concerning others. We are called to spread the word. Sometimes it's how I spread the word that backfires. Still, I will keep trying. If I don't try, I'll never know what works for one person and what works for another. What I can do is spread the word as best as I can. The rest is up to them.

MATHEW 10:14 And whosoever shall not receive you, nor hear your words, when ye depart out of that house or city, shake off the dust of your feet. Verily I say unto you, It shall be more tolerable for the land of Sodom and Gomorrha in the day of judgment, than for that city.

Does this mean that even though we are ***in*** the world, preaching the gospel, we should not be ***of*** the world? Far be it from me to try and interpret God's meaning and get it wrong. When I read the above passage, Mathew 10:14, that is my understanding. We must preach the gospel, but not take on the lifestyles of those who will not hear it.

MATHEW 9:28 And when he was come into the house, the blind men came to him: and Jesus saith unto them, Believe ye that I am able to do this? They said unto him, Yea, Lord. Then touched he their eyes, saying, According to your faith be it unto you. And their eyes were opened; and Jesus straitly charged them, saying, See that no man know it.

"According to your faith," might as well have been written in bright bold letters. What a powerful passage this is! Jesus asked them if they believed he could heal them. Then Jesus made the blind see because of their faith in God. "Yes!" they replied. Then the miracle that they asked for was granted. Their faith was the fuel to their request. They believed Jesus could heal them. Jesus did so. We can never take for granted the power of faith and the rewards God gives to the faithful.

MATHEW 10:28 And fear not them which kill the body, but are not able to kill the soul: but rather fear him which is able to destroy both soul and body in hell.

I cannot turn my back and look away from a tyrannical government. I cannot poke out my eyeballs and remain blind to what is happening in this world. Yet to combat evil, I need to remember what is most important in this quest for truth.

MATHEW 10:32 Whosoever therefore shall confess me before men, him will I confess also before my Father which is in Heaven. But whosoever shall deny me before men, him will I also deny before my Father which is in Heaven.

The Day of Judgment is coming. Repent and follow God as best you can. When you fall, repent. When you get back up, continue to praise the Lord. When you fall again...repent again. Don't try to condemn the Bible, just read it and try to understand it as best you can. When that fails, ask questions. Ask a pastor, ask a friend, ask anyone who will listen! Just remember that your life is not about ***you***, it is about serving God.

MATHEW 10:39 He that findeth his life shall lose it: and he that loseth his life for my sake shall find it.

We should follow Jesus Christ as is instructed in the Bible. We will not all come to this understanding at the same time in our lives. Some will figure this out sooner, some will not get it until their deathbed – the point is that whatever the case, you **must** find this understanding. If you are seeking it and still can't find it, have no fear. Pray about it. God knows when you are seeking him and cannot find him. He knows all. God will never give you more than you can handle. The most important thing you will do in your life is seek the Lord, Jesus Christ.

If I come off as 'preachy,' I apologize. It's just that this information is so important to me, I feel I have to repeat it constantly...more so, I'm not just being 'preachy' towards you, this is directed towards me as well. These are things *I* need to hear. This is information that *I* am seeking to understand.

EPHESIANS 5:1-2 Be ye therefore followers of God, as dear children; And walk in love, as Christ also hath loved us, and hath given himself for us an offering and a sacrifice to God for a sweet smelling savour.

CHAPTER ELEVEN
TEMPTATIONS

JAMES 1:13-14 Let no man say when he is tempted, I am tempted of God: for God cannot be tempted with evil, neither tempteth he any man: But every man is tempted, when he is drawn away of his own lust and enticed.

So, I guess I can't blame my temptations on God. I have to blame myself, for the most part. Only God knows what role the devil plays in tempting me. The devil did try to tempt Jesus, why would he not try to tempt a weak-minded soul like myself? The thing is, I will be tempted by things 'of my own lust.'

Isn't this also the premise of the book by J.R.R. Tolkien, **The Lord of the Rings**? The ring is a temptation to ones deepest desires. All who hold it are corrupted by evil. Those who use it become its slave. It cannot be destroyed but by the fire of Mount Doom, just as the devil cannot be destroyed until the end of days. The analogy is weak and flawed, but it is similar.

Martin Luther Speaks of Satan

"Satan may be overcome by contempt, but in faith, not in presumption. However, he is certainly not to be invited; for he is a powerful enemy, seeing and hearing everything that lies before us and that we are now talking about. And God permitting, he spoils everything that is good.

When the devil comes during the night to plague me, I give him this answer: "Devil, I must sleep now; for this is God's command: Work during the day, sleep at night." If he does not stop to vex me but faces me with my sins, I reply: "Dear devil, I have heard the record. But I have committed far more sins which do not even stand in your record. Put them down too..."

If he still does not stop accusing me as a sinner, I say to him in contempt: "Holy Satan, pray for me! You never have done anything evil and alone are holy. Go to God and acquire grace for yourself. If you want to make me righteous, I tell you: Physician heal yourself...

The devil has often raised a racket in the house and has tried to scare me, but I appealed to my calling and said, "I know that God has placed me into this house to be lord here. Now if you have a call that is stronger than mine and are lord here, then stay where you are. But I well know that you are not lord here and that you belong in a different place - down in hell." And so I fell asleep again and let him be angry, for I well knew that he could do nothing to me." - **Martin Luther**

Temptation

Temptation surrounds us every day. It's almost as if life is a tight rope we walk on. At any moment, the rope may break, or we may slip and fall. To walk a straight path with God is the greatest challenge you will ever face. I believe it is also the greatest journey one can travel on. To be tempted, to fail and keep walking on that tight rope is not as hard as it seems. The hard part is how to get back on that rope, once you have fallen off. Spiritual endurance is achieved through years of studying, learning, and grabbing a piece of wisdom from others. The core of this process, in my opinion, begins and ends with the Bible. Do I sound like a broken record yet?

Temptations

My mind has been tempted,
My body has been cold,
My brain feels so empty,
So I turn to my soul.
Look up into Heaven,
But never look down,
What we do unto others,
Will come back around.

I am learning to be humble. I am trying to be truthful within, in order to promote truth throughout. I have fallen many times, but each time that I fall I pick myself back up and continue on...

CHAPTER TWELVE
A FREE SOUL

Having the freedom to choose your faith and having a separation between church and state ensures that when you do seek out God, you do so because you want to.

Free Soul

Eternal is the soul,
Weak is the flesh,
If too hot or too cold,
then the body faces death,
The soul is a mystery,
The mind, too, is weak,
The body is fragile,
But the soul remains free.

"No one will enter the New World Order unless he or she will make a pledge to worship Lucifer. No one will enter the New Age unless he will take a Luciferian Initiation." – **David Spangler**, Director of Planetary Initiative, United Nations

Congress shall make no law respecting a religious establishment – 1st Amendment.

Some may see this amendment as anti-Christian but I see it as the opposite. Perhaps these people had so much faith that they did not wish for God to be used in their political spectrum as a tool. Instead, all people are free to choose their religion, or type of worship (Christianity), if they want any at all. Though politics is not above the realm of God, we should not use God to further our political 'ideals,' no matter how good the intention.

What is a free soul? What is the price of one's soul? What exactly the soul is remains a mystery. I believe every person should be free to choose their path in life. That means that people should be free to reject Christianity. Christianity doesn't work if it's forced. It requires free will to truly believe in God, in Jesus Christ, and in the Holy Spirit. I rejected

Christianity before I embraced it.

My Country

I don't want a religious country. I want a country that loves God because they *choose to do so*, not because they feel *pressured*. Still, I see a difference between God and religion. On the other hand, I consider myself a Christian. See how confusing simple things can be when we 'stereotype'? When we put people into little boxes in order to simplify them, we diminish the uniqueness we have within ourselves. We put ourselves into categories because it's easier than judging each person as an individual. Sometimes we go out of our way to shun the people that we do not understand. Sometimes we don't put in the effort to truly get to know a person. Sometimes we judge, even though we know we shouldn't.

Thou shall not judge.

Though I put God first, I should still try to follow the U.S. Constitution. To do so, however, I must learn about it and understand it in order to be able to share rational thoughts and opinions with others on this subject. I live to serve God. I'm on a spiritual journey. Yet the world does not stop spinning. There is a big difference between using politics to further the existence of God and using God to further your political agenda. I think both are dangerous. This is why free will is so important. It allows everyone the right to express their opinions. This means that people in politics can express religious views freely, just as people of faith or a religion can discuss politics freely. This doesn't mean that people should use their stature to force their views on others. Even Christ didn't do that.

Sometimes I confuse myself. Still, that's better than being confused by someone else. Especially from a man like Pat Robertson. Mr. Robertson has openly called for the assassination of foreign heads of state. What does that have to do with Christianity? Nothing. Is it freedom of speech? Perhaps. Is it immoral? That's in the eye of the beholder. A man like Pat Robertson is dangerous, for he can be vilified for saying something negative and then blasted across national TV for saying something positive.

During an interview with Susan Malveaux for CNN, December 23, 2008, Pat Robertson told her, "I am remarkably pleased with Obama. I had grave misgivings about him. But so help me, he's come in forcefully, intelligently. He's picked a middle of the road cabinet. And so far, if he continues down this course, he has the makings of a great president."

As Infowars.com journalist Kurt Nimmo writes, *"Obama's "middle of the road cabinet" consists of people hailing from the Council on Foreign Relations, the Trilateral Commission, and the secretive Bilderberg group. Timothy Geithner, Obama's pick to head up the Treasury, is* ***head of the Federal Reserve Bank of New York*** *and is the Fed's main liaison with Wall Street. Obama's so-called Economic Recovery Advisory Board will be chaired by former Federal Reserve Chairman Paul Volcker. Obama has outlined his geopolitical plans in Foreign Affairs, the mainstay periodical of the Council on Foreign Relations, and his wife, Michelle Obama, is a member of a branch of the CFR in Chicago."*

I don't know too many people who take Pat Robertson seriously. No one should charge for prayers. That's worse than money changers in front of a synagogue, in my opinion. I don't believe Obama has a middle of the road cabinet. More so, I have even less faith when it comes out of the mouth of Pat Robertson. It may be people like this who finally lead the sheep to the slaughter, just before the end of days. We'll see. I think that's why it's so important to create a one on one relationship with God. Relying on man will only bring disappointment. No one's perfect. Why try to be? Just be humble. I think that humility is a gift from God. In humility I am searching for my inner peace. It has been a long journey to get here. Now comes the hard part, staying in this mind frame. Things will come that will try to break my spirit and cause me to question my Christianity. So the fight continues. From now until the end of my life, it will continue. I cannot win, unless winning is believing in Jesus Christ and keeping the faith. I will only know if I have won ***that*** after I am gone from this world. I am free, yet I should be a servant to my fellow humans. I am blessed, yet I feel temptation every day of my life. I try to be humble, still sometimes I feel my pride being attacked. I have what I need, yet I still want. I am human.

"[North American Christians] have been insufficiently skeptical about the professed goodness of the US government and the professed independence of the mainstream [media] in America." - **David Ray Griffin**

Religion

We must show the world the beauty of Christianity, so that they may seek it out. Could you answer the Pharisees' questions better than Jesus? Of course not. Could you get close? Or would you stick your foot in your mouth as I often do? When you feel like you have been defeated in converting someone to Christianity, analyze the incident, asking yourself, "What did I do wrong?" This is better than writing the person off as a non-believer, for we were all non-believers once. My fellow Christians know the glory of God and the love of Jesus Christ. What else could you need? The separation among people that religion causes is counter-productive to Christianity itself. Religion forces us to choose which religion is right, therefore also choosing which religions are wrong, according to what the Bible says. Under these circumstances, it is hard to create unity among all of God's people. Having the freedom to choose your faith and having a separation between church and state ensures that when you do seek out God, you do so because you want to.

Religion can be manipulated easily. It is the greatest tool available to create division among God's people. Still, religion can be a beautiful thing, if used correctly. It's like fire. It can be used for cooking, for warmth, or for fuel. Yet fire can also burn you if you get too close. I often feel this same way about religion. I don't want to get too close, I just want to gain the knowledge I can use to further my journey and leave the rest in a pile of ashes. Jesus Christ unites. People divide. God loves. The devil deceives. God still loves. We screw up. God forgives. We search and find God through the Bible first. We search and find ourselves last.

I practice humility because I seek the truth, not my version of it.

I Value

I value myself,
As I value all others,
Showing love for my father,
My siblings and mother.
We're in this together,
Every one, every land,
In the beginning there was only,
One woman and one man.

CHAPTER THIRTEEN
THE FEAR

Mr. Schwartz was my journalism teacher at San Lorenzo High School. He taught me how to write a newspaper article and remain objective, neutral, and factual in it. He taught me the difference between journalists and columnists. A columnist writes opinion pieces. A journalist writes a story, using facts, eyewitnesses, past occurrences, and circumstantial evidence to present both sides of an argument. Rebuttals are very important. Collecting evidence and letting the reader decide was what hooked me to journalism. In this type of environment, it's hard to find unbiased media. Some journalists, editors, and columnists that do try to explore outside the realm of their 'charter' or mission statement do not last long in the realm of mainstream media. Usually they turn to the alternative media, where freedom still means something. The journalism class came to a screeching halt for me when I realize that most journalists spend a lot of time on the phone, taking notes and interviewing people. My stutter had always stopped me from going that extra distance. A lack of confidence, merged with my fears of embarrassment, kept me from being the best journalist I could be. There are just certain words and phrases that I can't say without stuttering. My stuttering involves a lot of blinking eyes and weird faces. So I usually just maneuver around any chance of this embarrassing moment.

"How could I be a journalist like this?" I thought. "I can't get on the phone and get the information I need. I'll be fearful of stuttering when interviewing people for my story." It just wasn't worth it. I figured if I wasn't going to be the best journalist I could be, there was no point in being a journalist at all. So while I finished my journalism class, my heart wasn't in it anymore. I still love journalism just as much as I enjoyed my drama class. Yet I can't foresee a time where I would return to either of those two. The fear of embarrassment kept me away from them, but it couldn't keep me away from writing. Whether it was news stories or plays, I still loved writing. No matter what happened in my life, I never stopped writing. As my life settled down, I began to write more and more. Yet the fears of my past still plagued me. When I saw my older brother performing live in front of people at the San Ramon Little Theater, I felt like I was right there with him. I had jitters on opening day. I kept asking myself, "What if...this? What if...that?" I was worried that he was going to stutter and people were going to laugh. Well, people did laugh but there were no stutters. I was so proud of him for getting over that fear. I am sure the reward was well worth those fearful feelings. It reminded me of when I was in a seventh grade play, based around Santa Claus. We were picking parts in my drama class when one paper happened to fall to the ground. I picked it up and read "Santa Claus," on the paper. I was playing Santa! Playing Santa helped me get over my stage fright. I actually had to sing in the play. I still remember the lines I sang:

"I, I, where have you wandered to?
You know, I am so fond of you,
Haven't I loved you and cherished and nourished you?
I won't you please come home."

The "I" was one of many letters other students played, together spelling out Christmas. Each student held a giant poster in front of their bodies, lining up to spell Christmas. For some reason, "I" had wandered off and the play focused on finding him. We performed it for the whole school. I remember looking out into the bleachers while on stage, and saw my mom, my two little sisters and my grandparents looking on with smiley faces. Having them there boosted my confidence. I wonder if my older brother, Manny, felt the same way when he was performing in "Harvey," last year. At least I only had to perform once. My brother would repeat his performance over the course of two weeks, four or five times overall. That is a great accomplishment. My own fears were used to find ways that I could use my vocal talents, without stuttering. When I found that music was the answer to my prayers, I ran with it. I could write a song, record it and perform it, all without stuttering. In the course of over twelve years of making music, I have never stuttered during this process. Never. I took it as a sign from God that I was on the right path. It was the content of the music that still needed work, but that would come later. It is not so important for me to do "whatever I want to do." It's more important to figure out what God wants me to do and follow that to the best of my ability. It is my life but I don't believe I'll find what I'm looking for unless I seek out God. There will be no fulfillment in life unless I seek God and the eternal question...why am I here? This journey far surpasses any other journey life could offer me. All I must be is willing to learn, to seek, to understand, and to believe in something greater than I, something that makes sense in an otherwise cruel and savage world.

CHAPTER FOURTEEN
GLOBAL EMPIRE

ROMANS 12:9-21 Love must be sincere. Hate what is evil; cling to what is good. Be devoted to one another in brotherly love. Honor one another above yourselves. Never be lacking in zeal, but keep your spiritual fervor, serving the Lord. Be joyful in hope, patient in affliction, faithful in prayer. Share with God's people who are in need. Practice hospitality.

Bless those who persecute you; bless and do not curse. Rejoice with those who rejoice; mourn with those who mourn. Live in harmony with one another. Do not be proud, but be willing to associate with people of low position. Do not be conceited. Do not repay anyone evil for evil. Be careful to do what is right in the eyes of everybody. If it is possible, as far as it depends on you, live at peace with everyone. Do not take revenge, my friends, but leave room for God's wrath, for it is written: "**It is mine to avenge; I will repay**," says the Lord. On the contrary:

"If your enemy is hungry, feed him; if he is thirsty, give him something to drink. In doing this, you will heap burning coals on his head." Do not be overcome by evil, but overcome evil with good.

"If leaders are serious about creating new global responsibilities *or governance*, let them start by modernizing multilateralism to empower the [World Trade Organization], the [International Monetary Fund], and the World Bank Group to *monitor national policies*." – **Robert Zoellick**, World Bank President

The Global Empire is emerging. Some are happily waiting, since the world has become so corrupt and so full of sin that they can see no other way but to unite the world under one global banner. In theory this may seem good, but there is one problem. "The Global Empire" that will be created will be done so by the same people who have ruined our world, under a different banner. We are giving 'the keys to the car' to the same people that totaled our vehicle! It doesn't make sense. Yet we did this with the bailout money as well. We give more power to banks, and more capitol to the Federal Reserve, hoping they will fix the problem they created. It doesn't work that way. Reform is not done so easily. If we forget about states sovereignty, and sovereign nations, we will eventually have a global empire. To do so, we have to get rid of the Constitution in the United States. I am one hundred percent opposed to this.

As Alex Jones says, "The government is out of control." Maybe that's because, like a corporation, the government has no conscious. There is little to no humanity in capitalism. There is less in corporatism. The government, as a whole, has proven to be worse. What do they want? Where does tyranny stop?

"I think a New World Order is emerging." – **Gordon Brown**, G-20 Summit, April 2009

Georgia On My Mind

In order to usher in a new world order, there has to be a virus, a plague, a mass terrorist incident, or some massive catastrophe on a global scale. In one word, *genocide.* There is a theory about population reduction to the amount of under 500,000,000. It's estimated that there are over 7 billion people (and growing) on the earth today. That statistic is about two years to three years old by the way. So the actual figures may be closer to 8 or 9 billion. Even at the lowest figures, that's a reduction of over 6 and a half billion people that would need to be eradicated.

The Georgia Guidestones claim that we humans need to "***Maintain Humanity under 500,000,000.***" It is unclear in mainstream news who created these stones and why? It ends by saying – "Be not a cancer on the earth, leave room for nature, leave room for nature." In order to maintain a population of under 500,000,000 people...you would have to reduce population through population control. In other words, back door murder:

- Cancer
- Pollution
- Diseases
- Abortion
- Sacrifice
- Murder (Iraq & Afghanistan)
- Genocide - Rwanda, Nazi Germany, Kosovo, ect.

In the pyramid of evil, we must think about these things, even if we are to leave other people to actually "deal" with these problems.

WWJD? What would Jesus do? I have no idea. I only know what Greg can and can't do. What I *can't* do, is to do nothing. I can always do something. As I discussed with my friend German, just talking about these things is doing *something*. Ignorance is not an option for me. So I have to work through my ignorance, fight off distractions and try to learn about world events as much as I can. I have to fight the evil that tells me to look the other way, and says, "That's not your problem, Greg."

I am a man of slow action, cautious action. If it be God's will, I will take action, in many ways. The Georgia Guide stones mysteriously stand in Georgia, Elbert County. Less than a hundred miles from Atlanta, these stones quietly act as a 'manifesto' for human civilization. Why are they here? Who put them here? It's unclear to me at this point. If you're ever driving down Hartwell Highway, Georgia Highway 77, look out the window and you may see the guide stones in the distance. Follow the signs that indicate the turn-off that takes you to the Guide stones. Look for the street sign, "Guide stones Road."

Wikapedia.com states: *According to the Georgia Mountain Travel Association's detailed history: "The Georgia Guide stones are located on the farm of Mildred and Wayne Mullenix...The Elbert County land registration system shows what appears to be the Guidestones as County land purchased on October 1, 1979."*

Mark Dice, of MarkDice.com, explained that the guide stones should "be smashed into a million pieces, and then the rubble used for a construction project." Like myself, Mark believes that the guide stones have "a deep Satanic origin." At the unveiling of the monument, a local minister proclaimed that he believed the monument was "for sun worshipers, for cult worship and for devil worship." (source: wikapedia.com) Take it for what it's worth, but population reduction can only be achieved by genocide, various forms of murders, and toxins and chemicals that plague the earth. As I believe, all these evils come from the same source. In a deeper sense, everything comes from God, the creator. But through free will, or something that I don't understand, Satan has been given reign over the world and humans have been given a choice to believe in God or not. Nothing I can do or say will make you believe in God. You must look within yourself. That is where you will find God. Look in your soul.

God is here, there, and everywhere – all around you. When Yoda was talking about "the force" in Star Wars: The Empire Strikes Back, he might as well have been talking about God. "For my ally is the Force. And a powerful ally it is...It's energy surrounds us and binds us. Luminous beings are we...(Yoda pinches Luke's shoulder)...not this crude matter. You must feel the Force around you. Here, between you...me...the tree...the rock...everywhere! Yes, even between this land and that ship!"

Back to the real world...God is waiting for you to let him into your heart, your mind, your body, and your soul. So what are you waiting for? Haven't you heard the good news? *He has risen!*

CHAPTER FIFTEEN
FALL OF HUMANITY

Up And Away

I look up to Heaven and what do I see?
Billions and Trillions of people,
who are all just like me...
My life is a mystery,
My book yet unfinished,
I am tempted and sinful,
But never diminished,
My faith is a rock,
My spirit is with me,
Redemption, salvation,
From a God who's forgiving.

There has been a fall of humanity, just as there also has been, as the Alex Jones movie is titled, a "Fall of the Republic." Sometimes people cringe when I say Bible, God, morals, values, Christianity, and the one that causes people to roll their eyes, while slightly titling their head...Jesus Christ. I wonder where the fall of humanity began. Did it begin in Heaven? Was it when Satan *fell* because Satan wanted to be God? Was it when Adam and Eve *fell* victims to temptations "of their own lusts?" Was it when humans *fell*, by killing Jesus Christ? Humanity has fallen from what it once was, over and over again, throughout history.

Fall Of The Republic

From Infowars.com: *Fall Of The Republic has exploded onto the Internet as millions of people worldwide take the red pill and discover the antidote to the establishment's lies about what caused the financial collapse and their agenda to deceptively claim that empowering the very culprits of the crime will solve the problem, as America is frog-marched into a tyrannical system of world government.*

The Obama Deception receiving tens of millions of views, early indications just over a week after the film was released are that this indeed happening. The You Tube version below already has over 300,000 views and this is just one of thousands of different versions that are floating around the web. The entire project behind producing the film cost hundreds of thousands of dollars, but the information contained in the movie is so important to communicate and the times so perilous that we want as many people to see this documentary as possible, whether they pay for it or not – this is our main mission. (Source: Fall of the Republic: Millions of People Worldwide Take the Red Pill" Paul Joseph Watson, PrisonPlanet.com, Friday, October 30, 2009)

What does this have to do with spirituality? For you it may have nothing to do with it. For me, it's all related. I began a journey to learn about false flag terrorism and ended up where I should have been all along, seeking God for the answers to life's mysteries. Though we all have free will, I truly believe that God has already laid out a path for us to follow. Our free will decides how we get there, but God decides where we go. I believe it is the devil that has put man against man, religion against religion. A spiritual relationship with God cannot be contained in any one religion, let alone the many religious sects within the particular belief. I began researching 9/11 and the Iraq War as two separate events that had nothing to do with each other, other than Bush's claims of ties between Osama bin Laden and Saddam Hussein. Beyond that, I could see no connection. Yet there was and is a strong connection between the two events. They are *somewhat* related; that is, if you believe that there is a global domination conspiracy, also known as the new world order, the Bilderberg Group, off-shore bankers, the shadow government and the "Global Empire." All these groups are inner-connected at certain levels.

There are many names for the 'one world connection.' Is it so hard to believe that the evils and the corruptions of this world have been orchestrated all along? In a spiritual sense, this is the work of the devil. The further I researched these two events, the more the same players kept popping up. My curiosity rose to an all time high...is this really happening? If so, how do I fight this evil? As I have learned over the years, when I'm in trouble or when I'm in need I turn to God for help. I know that evil days are upon us. Yet I feel I must do something, anything to combat evil. So where do I turn to? The scriptures. In the Bible, the teachings of Jesus Christ give me hope for a future. The world is not all doom and gloom when you have God in your heart. The more I read the book of Mathew, Mark, Luke, and John, the more I see how Jesus Christ has fought evil. It wasn't through violence that people turned to Christ. It was the miracles, the preachings, and the compassion he had for the people that kept them amazed by his glory.

MATHEW 15:32 Then Jesus called his disciples unto him, and said, **I have compassion on the multitude, because they continue with me now three days, and have nothing to eat: and I will not send them away fasting, lest they faint in the way.**

The multitude that followed Jesus Christ over two thousand years ago has been growing and continues to grow to this day. Every waking day, someone receives the Lord into their heart. Someone decides to give their life over to Jesus Christ, knowing this is not the end, it is only the beginning of a life long journey of serving God. Think about how many people since the days Jesus walked the earth have been following him, generation after generation. One after another, people are seeking and finding Jesus Christ. Wars come and go, people die all the time, but what remains eternal is Jesus Christ. Even after death, the Christ and his influence continues to grow stronger every day. The more people are persecuted by other people, the more they run to God, seeking shelter. From the time he began preaching to the people, and to this very day, Jesus has been gathering his sheep, so one day they will return home with him. I want to be one of the people in the multitudes that Jesus will show compassion for. So I must seek him out. Anyone who truly seeks how to look up to Heaven should be looking in the Bible first. Since the devil is constantly trying to confuse us, we must combat this evil with knowledge of the Bible. Here we find how Jesus dealt with the temptations of the evil one and overcame it all. Of course we cannot be God or deal with evil as God did, but we can learn from these scriptures and see how Jesus was able to combat Satan. Jesus was tempted by Satan, just as we are every day of our lives.

MATHEW 4:3 The tempter came to him and said, "If you are the Son of God, tell these stones to become bread." Jesus answered, "**It is written: 'Man does not live on bread alone, but on every word that comes from the mouth of God**.'" Then the devil took him to the holy city and had him stand on the highest point of the temple. "If you are the Son of God," he said, "throw yourself down. For it is written: "'He will command his angels concerning you, and they will lift you up in their hands, so that you will not strike your foot against a stone.'" Jesus answered him, "**It is**

also written: 'Do not put the Lord your God to the test.'" Again, the devil took him to a very high mountain and showed him all the kingdoms of the world and their splendor. "All this I will give you," he said, "if you will bow down and worship me." Jesus said to him, "**Away from me, Satan! For it is written: 'Worship the Lord your God, and serve him only**.'" Then the devil left him, and angels came and attended him.

The first time I read the book of Mathew, I was deeply moved by how Jesus Christ handled the devil, the tempter. The calm way Jesus spoke assured me that if what I sought was eternal peace, then through the teachings of Jesus Christ, I would eventually get there. I do believe that eternal peace will come after Judgment Day. The Lord calls on us to be ready for the day of judgment. At any time, Christ may return. Am I ready? I don't know. Only God knows. All I can do is try. Try to understand the word of God, try to read the Bible, try to follow God's commandments, try to show compassion and mercy as Jesus did, and try to be a better person. It's hard to follow the Bible if you're not reading it. So pick it up as much as you can! Get a version that is easily understandable to you. The New International Version of the Bible was where I began. Had I began with the King James Version, I think a lot of information would have went straight over my head. Whatever you do, follow God! Seek out Jesus Christ and you will see how you can be a better person to yourself and to those around you.

ROMANS 14:13-21 Therefore let us stop passing judgment on one another. Instead, make up your mind not to put any stumbling block or obstacle in your brother's way. As one who is in the Lord Jesus, I am fully convinced that no food is unclean in itself. But if anyone regards something as unclean, then for him it is unclean. If your brother is distressed because of what you eat, you are no longer acting in love. Do not by your eating destroy your brother for whom Christ died. Do not allow what you consider good to be spoken of as evil. For the kingdom of God is not a matter of eating and drinking, but of righteousness, peace and joy in the Holy Spirit, because anyone who serves Christ in this way is pleasing to God and approved by men. Let us therefore make every effort to do what leads to peace and to mutual edification. Do not destroy the work of God for the sake of food. All food is clean, but it is wrong for a man to eat anything that causes someone else to stumble. It is better not to eat meat or drink wine or to do anything else that will cause your brother to fall.

CONCLUSION

JOHN 20:21 Then Jesus said to them again, **Peace be unto you: as my Father hath sent me, even so send I you.**

JOHN 20:24-25 But Thomas, one of the twelve...was not with them when Jesus came. The other disciples therefore said unto him. We have seen the Lord. But he said unto them 'Except I shall see in his hands the print of the nails, and put my finger into the print of the nails and thrust my hand into his side, I will not believe.'

Even after everything Jesus Christ had done, after all the miracles and wonders that Jesus did for the people, and even though so many followed the Christ, Thomas still had his doubts. Even after Jesus Christ fed people by the thousands on a few pieces of fish and bread, Thomas still did not believe what Jesus foretold and he would not believe until he saw Jesus with his own eyes. Knowing what was in the mind of Thomas, the Lord granted his request.

JOHN 20:26-29 And after eight days again his disciples were within, and Thomas with them: then came Jesus, the doors being shut, and stood in the midst, and said, **Peace be unto you**. Then saith he to Thomas, **Reach hither thy finger, and behold my hands; and reach hither thy hand, and thrust it into my side: and be not faithless, but believing**. And Thomas answered and said unto him, My Lord and my God. Jesus saith unto him, **Thomas, because thou hast seen me, thou hast believed: blessed are they that have not seen, and yet have believed**.

That is a powerful message about faith. Seeing was believing for Thomas. Those of us who have not seen the Christ and still believe have to rely on faith, the Bible, and gained knowledge. These are powerful tools in seeking out God and understanding what it is that the good Lord has planned for you. The tools are at your disposal. All you have to do is use them.

ACTS 1:7-11 And he said unto them, It is not for you to know the times or the seasons, which the Father hath put in his own power. But ye shall receive power, after that the Holy Ghost is come upon you: and ye shall be witnesses unto me both in Jerusalem, and in all Judaea, and in Samaria, and unto the uttermost part of the earth. And when he had spoken these things, while they beheld, he was taken up; and a cloud received him out of their sight. And while they looked stedfastly toward Heaven as he went up, behold, two men stood by them in white apparel; Which also said, Ye men of Galilee, why stand ye gazing up into Heaven? This same Jesus, which is taken up from you into Heaven, shall so come in like manner as ye have seen him go into Heaven.

So I continue to look up to Heaven, waiting for the return of our God. Though sometimes we feel like we're doing *nothing*, we may be doing God's work, without even knowing it. "It's about nothing!" Yet even nothing is something. However many questions I have about the 9/11 conspiracy, the questions quadruple when it comes to spirituality. What is spirituality? How can society put it in a nice little box of generic stereo types? It cannot be done without some major flaws. So when that box is opened and all the gaps and holes have caused the good information to seep out, what are you left with? "Nothing."

"There's a show, that's a show." Yet the show is weak, like a reality television show. It's half true that reality shows display reality. It's fake reality and a fake television show. So to me, reality shows are about nothing.

What is spirituality? Why am I fighting so hard to distance myself from the word "Religion?" The Bible itself is bigger than religion. It is universal. The Bible is a beautiful book full of God's laws, human history, life lessons, and miracles and wonders. Yet it can be manipulated and corrupted. If you corrupt Gods children by perverting the Bible, do not forget to beg for mercy when you meet the creator. As I believe, it is never too late to repent and only God knows who is going to Heaven and who will be looking up to Heaven forever. Are you having a hard time distinguishing religion from spirituality? In my heart, I believe there is a big difference. I also believe that whatever brings you closer to God is a good thing. *I know where I am at now. I know where I want to be in life. Yet, is that where God wants me to be?*

Looking up to Heaven

The birds do 'chirp,'
And the Angels sing,
Are humans like angels,
Who lost all their wings?
I look up in search,
I look up to ponder,
I pray and I wait,
Till my spirit is stronger.

It has been a long and windy road in this thing we call life. Before we know it, we're almost out the door and on our way to Heaven. What matters is what we do while we're here. Our works on earth will be judged by the only one who has the authority to judge, the Lord Jesus Christ. You can call God any name you want, just as long as you call on him when times are tough.

To try to be God or to ignore God is very dangerous. Lucifer tried to be God. When that didn't work, he tried to pervert God's people. That will not work either. The pride of the evil one will not last forever, for one day, even the evil one will bow before God. One day, we will all be judged.

Yet there is hope. Salvation is right around the corner! All you must be is *willing*. If you are willing to try and understand what purpose God has for you, your eyes will open as they have never before. The energy and strength that God has placed inside of you awakens and your true search begins. We know where it ends – so what will you do to try and spread positive influences while you're here?

I leave that to you to decide. What does spirituality mean to you and why?

THE END

Jesus is the way to salvation. The Bible is the word of God. We cannot take away or add to the Bible. It is complete. Jesus has risen. To God be the glory! Forever and ever. Amen.

Thank you for your support. ***From the tree of money, you pick cash. From the tree of knowledge, you pick wisdom. Which is worth more?***

www.ingramcontent.com/pod-product-compliance
Ingram Content Group UK Ltd.
Pitfield, Milton Keynes, MK11 3LW, UK
UKHW041920190726
13854UKWH00003B/1347